Being and

Insurrection

CANNAE
PRESS

Being and Insurrection

Existential Liberation Critique, Sketches and Ruptures

A. Shahid Stover

O Son of Spirit!

The best beloved of all things in My sight is Justice; turn not away therefrom if thou desirest Me, neglect it not that I may confide in thee. By its aid thou shalt see with thine own eyes and not through the eyes of others, and shalt know of thine own knowledge and not through the knowledge of thy neighbor. Ponder this in thy heart how it behooveth thee to be. Verily justice is My gift to thee and the sign of My loving-kindness. Set it then before thine eyes.[1]

-Baha'u'llah (1817-1892)

[1] Baha'u'llah, *Writings of Baha'u'llah: A Compilation*, (New Delhi: Bahai Publishing Trust, 2006) p.41.

Dedicated to Nardi and Tadeos
for such
Love and Endurance

Much respect to *The Brotherwise Dispatch* editorial cipher – Sultan Stover, Dario Sanchez-Kennedy and Robert J. Jackson.

And much appreciation in particular to LaRose T. Parris and David L. Schalk for their close, careful and critical readings of this work.

A. Shahid Stover

Being and Insurrection

Existential Liberation Critique, Sketches and Ruptures

CANNAE
PRESS

New York

0 5 2 3 1 8 4 4 1

Published by
Cannae Press
P.O. Box 460
New York, NY 10276
cannaepress.com

Cover Design and Illustration by VC Design Studios
vcdesignstudios.com

Library of Congress Control Number: 2018915304
ISBN: 978-1-7335510-0-7 (paperback)
ISBN: 978-1-7335510-1-4 (ebook)

****

Contents

Contents

Preface

Black liberation discourse provides an insurgent cutting edge to the radical imagination precisely because the normative gaze of Empire which seeks to render it incongruous, is hegemonic. Does not the entire biopolitical impetus of *chattel* slavery, which historically subsidizes modernity itself, rest upon the violent systematic pacification of human 'being' into 'objecthood'? This imposition of 'objecthood' reveals the extent to which the irreducible agency of our human condition is structurally coerced and rationally regulated to cede human subjectivity by behaviorally embracing an explicit biological determinism that socially coalesces into materialist significations of 'race'.

As such, 'race' substantiates dehumanizing violence as an ahistorical harmony that positions western imperialist power as ultimate authority and arbiter of the Real. Insurgent philosophy thus interrogates the Real and enunciates Revolt, introducing ruptures against the normative gaze as discursive openings towards emancipatory praxis.

As an unapologetic work of insurgent philosophy, *Being and Insurrection* unites free flowing essays, aphoristic sketches and epistemological ruptures into an unrelenting polemic against the biopolitical pacification of human agency by a western imperialist continuum. This aesthetic unity of radical theory and fragmentary elucidation positions thought to resist the merciless efficiency with which established structures of meaning inevitably attempt to assimilate opposition and neutralize antagonisms. Although the density of insurgent philosophical prose places significant demands upon the reader, it is precisely this insistence that discloses a horizon of discursive potentialities that sword against conventional modes of analysis which claim to render thought digestible only to mask an unencumbered collusion with established power.

The particular writings that comprise this work reveal an explicit existential liberationist turn in my ongoing intellectual endeavors and are primarily drawn and revised from my discursive contributions from 2009 through 2018 to *The Brotherwise Dispatch*, a quarterly journal of radical theory, social critiques and emancipatory aesthetics that I started in 2001 and have been publishing ever since.

Existential liberation critique interrogates the Real and enunciates Revolt through lived Black experience, exploring the dialectic relation between our perception of the human condition and its dynamic influence on how we conceive socio-historical possibilities of human liberation. Does not the horizon of emancipatory praxis ultimately coincide with an ontological wager placed on just what exactly constitutes human 'being'? As such, with *Being and Insurrection*, existential liberation critique comes into its own as a decisive heuristic method and un-restrained hermeneutic orientation of insurgent philosophy informed by the anti-slavery dialectic of Frederick Douglass, the existential Marxism of Jean-Paul Sartre and the decolonial phenomenology of Frantz Fanon.[2]

And yet, is there a method of philosophical inquiry that prepares one for wrestling with the sheer gravity of Empire's normative gaze; a gaze that is constituted through the structural-inert violence and miseducation of soul which gravely overdetermines lived Black experience from without? In what sense do the murders of DeAndre Joshua, Darren Seals and Edward Crawford speak to a systematic accumulative slaughter of human 'being'? What do the insurrections of Tottenham, Ferguson and Baltimore tell us about a lived coloniality that

---

[2] Lewis R. Gordon's *Fanon and the Crisis of European Man*, (New York: Routledge, 1995) and *Existentia Africana*, (New York: Routledge, 2000), Mark Poster's *Existential Marxism in Postwar France*, (Princeton: Princeton University Press, 1975), Frank B. Wilderson III's "The Prison Slave as Hegemony's (Silent) Scandal" in *Social Justice*, Vol.20, No.2, 2003 and "Gramsci's Black Marx: Whither the Slave in Civil Society?" in *Social Identities*, Vol.9, No.2, 2003, and Thomas R. Flynn's *Sartre and Marxist Existentialism*, (Chicago: University of Chicago Press, 1984) serve as important preliminary catalysts towards the eventual theoretical development and philosophical articulation of existential liberation theory.

binds the imperial mainstream-as-civil society to the socio-ontological underground of modernity with a totalitarian coherence? No doubt, the dynamic atmosphere of massive protests and spontaneous rebellions intermittently engulfing the world does more than any possible theory, or philosophy, to render our current era of social turmoil geohistorically visible, not as information or facts, but as reservoirs of meaning from which to interrogate the Real and enunciate Revolt.

Nonetheless, intellectual endeavor is not a form of abstinence from action; rather it is a lived rhythm of praxis as a singular mode of 'being-in-the-world' which implicates us in relation to the global scope of established power and the ideological currents that inundate every frontier of human existence.

As such, this work includes philosophical provocations involving the ever controversial 'N-word', the obsolescence of Freudian anthropology and the emancipatory potentialities of Art. These provocations aim to introduce epistemological disequilibrium within established structures of meaning towards resisting contemporary reconfigurations of racist dehumanization into a sovereign legitimacy of Empire.

Indeed, the exceptional antagonism against western imperialist power that originates in the assertion of Black subjectivity-as-human 'being' cannot be stilled by attempts to anthropologically quarantine the radical imagination within the normative gaze. And thus, I choose to write, even as onrushing crises overwhelm the pen, and the Molotov cocktail never ceases to beckon . . .

the normative gaze, lived Black experience and Empire
– The normative gaze[3] renders a western imperialist
continuum coherent unto itself through objective
violence and miseducation of soul, thus constituting
hegemony through the topographical legitimation
of coloniality.[4]   In organizing social consciousness
and sanctioning ahistorical memory towards an unreflective public constellation of values, standards
and narratives, the normative gaze ideologically
veils the concerted praxis and systematic imperatives of globalized structural-inert power with a

---

[3] Early philosophical engagements with the normative gaze can be
found in the work of Frederick Douglass, "it is necessary to resort
to these cruelties, in order to make the slave a slave, and to keep
him a slave . . . and this can be done only by shutting out the light
of education from their minds and brutalizing their persons." *The
Life and Writings of Frederick Douglass Vol.1*, (New York:
International Publishers, 1846, 1950) p.157, and W.E.B. DuBois
through his emphasis on 'double consciousness' in *The Souls of
Black Folk*, (New York: Dover, 1903, 1994). However, Cornel
West initiates the conceptual formulation of the term "normative
gaze" towards an insurgent philosophical discourse in "The
Genealogy of Modern Racism", *Prophesy Deliverance!*,
(Philadelphia: Westminster Press, 1982) p.53.
[4] Although theoretical antecedents grappling with coloniality are
found in the work of W.E.B. DuBois, Jean-Paul Sartre, Frantz
Fanon, Harold Cruse and Eldridge Cleaver, it is Anibal Quijano
who ushers in its explicit conceptual breakthrough. See
"Coloniality of Power, Eurocentrism and Latin America",
Nepantla: Views from the South 1.3, included in *Coloniality At
Large*, edited by Mabel Morana, Enrique Dussel, and Carlos A.
Jauregui, (Durham: Duke University Press, 2008), see also *The
Brotherwise Dispatch* Vol.2, #17, Sept-Nov/2015.

disinterested existential legitimacy as arbitrary circumstances of the Real.

And yet, the normative gaze is not solely an "ideal from which to order and compare observations",[5] nor should it be reduced to a rational consensus of interests, for it arises as the epistemological correlate of established power functioning as the Real of absolute authority outside any dependence upon intersubjective resonance, thus imposing itself upon social interactions. Indeed, the normative gaze is ignored only at great consequence to authentic 'being-in-the-world'.

By preempting both the enunciation of spontaneous thought in ordinary discourse and the articulation of formal rationality in academia, the normative gaze constitutes objective truth as an intervention of materiality upon human agency, mediating against the constitutive self-determination, relentless transcendence and spiritual upheaval of human 'being'.

Abdicating the irreducibility of human agency to the normative gaze promotes conditions for achieving a substantive identity anchored in stable positionality to the imperial mainstream of modernity.[6]

---

[5] Cornel West, *Prophesy Deliverance!*, p.54.

[6] "Modernity is born when Europe (the peripheral Europe of the Muslim and Ottoman world), begins its expansion beyond its historical limits. Europe arrives in Africa; in India and Japan, thanks to Portugal; in Latin America, and from there to the

In contrast, human subjectivity is predicated solely upon a lived rhythm of praxis as spiritual resistance of human 'being' to this overdetermination-from-without that is subsidized by structural-inert violence and miseducation of soul. Therefore, the normative gaze, as reflexivity of established power imposing the Real upon situated consciousness, operates irrespective of intersubjective modalities of consent or dissent, existing as a sword suspended by a thread over lived Black experience. For "racism has to become a practice: it is not contemplation awakening the significations engraved on things; it is in itself self-justifying violence: violence presenting itself as induced violence, counter-violence and legitimate defense."[7]

Indeed, the phenomenon of lived Black experience discloses the normative gaze of a western imperialist continuum which yields "no true self-consciousness, but only lets him see himself through the

---

Philippines, thanks to the Spanish conquest. That is to say, Europe has become itself 'center.' The other races and cultures now appear as 'immature,' barbarous, underdeveloped. . . . And lastly, the victims of modernity in the periphery (the extermination of the indians, the enslavement of the Africans, the colonization of the Asians) and in the center (the genocide of Jews, the third holocaust) are the "responsible" ones for their own victimization." Enrique Dussel, *The Underside of Modernity*, (Atlantic Highlands, New Jersey: Humanities Press, 1996) p.52.

[7] Jean-Paul Sartre, *Critique of Dialectical Reason Vol.1*, (London: Verso, 1960, 1991) p.720.

revelation of the other world"[8] as an "object in the midst of other objects",[9] rendering naked a profound abdication of human subjectivity as the anthropological correlate of Empire.

And yet, against imperialist structures of meaning[10] attempting to suffocate our ascendant humanity, suppressing our capacity to disclose the Real of

---

[8] DuBois, *The Souls of Black Folk*, p.2.

[9] Frantz Fanon, *Black Skin, White Masks*, (New York: Grove Press, 1952, 1967) p.109.

[10] "It concerns a fundamental arrangement of knowledge, which orders the knowledge of beings so as to make it possible to represent them in a system of names. There were doubtless, in this region we now term life, many inquiries other than attempts at classification, many kinds of analysis other than that of identities and differences. But they all rested upon a sort of historical a priori, which authorized them in their dispersion and in their singular and divergent projects, and rendered equally possible all the differences of opinion of which they were the source. This a priori does not consist of a set of constant problems uninterruptedly presented to men's curiosity by concrete phenomena as so many enigmas; nor is it made up of a certain state of acquired knowledge laid down in the course of the preceding ages and providing a ground for the more or less irregular, more or less rapid, progress of rationality; it is doubtless not even determined by what is called the mentality or the 'framework of thought' of any given period, if we are to understand by that the historical outline of the speculative interests, beliefs, or broad theoretical options of the time. This a priori is what, in a given period, delimits in the totality of experience a field of knowledge, defines the mode of being of the objects that appear in that field, provides man's everyday perception with theoretical powers, and defines the conditions in which he can sustain a discourse about things that is recognized to be true." Michel Foucault, *The Order of Things*, (New York: Vintage, 1966, 1994) p.157-8.

contemporary human suffering under the weight of established power: we choose to cultivate our all too human voice precisely by speaking loudly, in an unruly manner, and completely out of turn, with a demeanor still simmering from historical injustice, ready at the slightest provocation to boil over into a discursive melee, or social incident.

Against the dread virus of repressive neo-colonial police presence which infects consciousness and inoculates communities of human 'being' with a violent omniscience that seeks to silence dissent and contravene socio-historical rebellion at its most nascent ontological and organic expressions: every autonomous thought, every emancipatory gaze at a police agent, every middle finger directed at a politician, every 'uncouth' projection of Black masculine bravado, and every semiotic 'irrational' expression of Black feminine attitude in the public sphere is indicative of cultural dispositions as persistent and invaluable challenges to unjust authority.

Against the gravity of biopolitical danger that permanently fixes and materially prefigures our guilt before we carry out a single act, when even the mere assertion of our human agency inspires perpetual criminalization: is it any wonder why we often choose to reject the dehumanizing premise, and test the imperial parameters of legality as suggested by globalized structural-inert power?

Against the counterinsurgent dictates of 'law and order' that murder, hound, torture, harass and systematically quarantine *the wretched of the earth*[11] within a vast prison industrial complex, hence fueling mass incarceration and immigrant internment: we experience 'being-in-the-world' as socio-ontological fugitives on the run from an omnipresent neo-colonial surveillance apparatus which sees, documents and records everything imaginable, with the exception of our Black subjectivity-as-human 'being'. "Racism, as a function of extraordinary individuals conceals the structural dimension of a society that conceals itself from itself through making its noxious values so familiar and frequent that they cease to function as objects of observation and reflection; they, in short, become unreflective and so steeped in familiarity that they become invisible."[12] Indeed, under the normative gaze of western imperialist power, the human condition exists in coercive anonymity.

---

[11] Frantz Fanon, *The Wretched of the Earth*, (Grove Press: New York, 1961, 1963).

[12] Lewis R. Gordon, *Fanon and the Crisis of European Man*, p.38.

situated consciousness (ain't a damn 'thing') – Human 'being' discloses an irrefutable dynamic of existence as 'no-thing-ness', defining the human condition as irreducible agency of situated consciousness that is irreconcilable with the Real and thus indistinguishable from being free.[13] And yet, though born through Woman's labor into socio-historical conditions beyond our control that ultimately situate human 'being', it remains within our decisive responsibility to cultivate human subjectivity out of a lived rhythm of praxis that correlates the irreducibility of human agency and its irreconcilability with the Real.

For the Real, as exhaustive tangible materiality of existence, exerts a severity of ontological gravity upon praxis – overwhelming human agency, situating consciousness as continuous project, mediating our spontaneity and implicating our temporality.

Indeed, human 'being' introduces a lived rhythm of praxis into existence, as the prominence of constitutive self-determination, relentless transcendence

---

[13] "Such is the truth of man's right to liberty. It existed in the very idea of man's creation. It was *his* even before he comprehended it. He was created in it, endowed with it, and it can never be taken from him. . . . The existence of this right is self-evident. It is written upon all the powers and faculties of man." Frederick Douglass, "Lecture on Slavery", *The Life and Writings of Frederick Douglass Vol.2*, p.140.

"Man does not exist *first* in order to be free *subsequently*; there is no difference between the being of man and his *being-free*." Jean-Paul Sartre, *Being and Nothingness*, (New York: Washington Square Press, 1956) p.60.

and spiritual upheaval experienced through a kinetic distance of interiority or 'presence-towards-self'[14] that characterizes consciousness venturing forth towards the world and actualizing itself in distinction and sharp relief against the concrete significance of the Real.

As such, 'being-in-the-world' as an authentic engagement, resists the Real through lived rhythm of praxis[15] and discloses an ontological reliance upon the prowess of our interrogation, perception and inspiration that binds existence as an open dialectic movement of call and response that mediates between human 'being' and the world.

Human 'being' thus unites reverberations of meaning and brings forth the very conditions of possibility for one to conceive of that affective totality of implicated temporality and socio-historical situation which is understood as 'the world'. Constitutive self-determination compels human 'being' as radical undertaking towards the world and intersubjective resonance towards one another, hence cultivating human subjectivity through praxis as

---

[14] "Man is free because there is no self, only a presence-to-self." Sartre, *Being and Nothingness*, p.568. Modified translation my own.

[15] "Praxis constantly reshapes the order of exteriority on the basis of a deeper unity." Sartre, *Critique of Dialectical Reason Vol.1*, p.87.

lived consistency of meaning in tireless dialectic movement against the socio-ontological weight of nature, culture and historical situation. "Man is motion toward the world and toward his like."[16] Such unabated dialectic movement resists the onto-logical gravity of assimilation with the Real and dis-closes constitutive potentialities of human 'being' as soulfully commensurate with a frenetic breakbeat of relentless transcendence; consciousness continuous-ly surpassing the situated present, and a steady bassline of spiritual upheaval; consciousness perpe-tually uprooting from the constituted past.

The human condition is therefore not authen-tically experienced as an evolutionary neurobio-logical determinism of rational animality, or as the causal immanence of a substantive 'empirical self', but lived as a rhythm of praxis, an intentional traj-ectory of situated consciousness fully capable of resisting the gravitational circumference of the Real; in spite of being thoroughly implicated by the sheer temporality of existence and facticity of history. This radical ontological movement of explicit refer-ential consciousness is inexorably one with implicit non-referential consciousness, an undifferentiated venture of intentionality as renunciation and affir-

---

[16] Fanon, *Black Skin, White Masks*, p.41.

mation.[17] "All that there is of intention in my actual consciousness is directed toward the outside, toward the world. In turn, this spontaneous consciousness of my perception is constitutive of my perceptive consciousness. In other words, every positional consciousness of an object is at the same time a non-positional consciousness of itself."[18] Indeed, renunciation of accumulated referential everyday social adjustments and cultural accommodations to the normative gaze of established power simultaneously discloses affirmation of a non-referential kinetic distance of interiority as spiritual autonomy, as 'presence-towards-self', as situated consciousness indicative of 'being-in-the-world'.

Thus, the open dialectic of call and response that characterizes human 'being' engaged with history through lived rhythm of praxis as radical undertaking towards the world and intersubjective resonance towards one another, need not ontologically yield to a reified anthropology inherited from structural-inert global power which overdetermines lived experience from without. This overdetermination-from-without encourages abdication of the human condition to an anthropological triumph of sedentary materialist determinism embodied in an 'empirical self-as-rational animality',

---

[17] "man is a *yes*. I will never stop reiterating that. . . . But man is also a *no.*" Fanon, p.222.
[18] Sartre, *Being and Nothingness*, p.12-13.

which effortlessly coalesces with the normative gaze of a western imperialist continuum.

To resist such overdetermination-from-without actualizes spiritual autonomy as 'presence-towards-self' against the numbing hegemony of established power. This resistance originates through lived rhythm of praxis encompassing kinetic recognition towards the Divine as transcendent horizon of meaning. For the very assertion of the irreducible agency of human 'being' and its irreconcilability with the Real, as lived rhythm of praxis towards the Divine, pierces through veils of 'objecthood' and undermines the epistemologically tempting deceptions of a concrete 'empirical self', thereby initiating dynamics of interiority as implicit kinetic distance of constitutive self-determination, relentless transcendence and spiritual upheaval – thus unchaining human subjectivity from bondage to materialist determinism, and bearing witness to an abiding radical ontological freedom and lived prominence of the human condition as situated consciousness.

being-towards-the Divine – Human subjectivity as 'being-towards-the Divine', discloses the unceasing genesis of human subjectivity constituted through lived rhythm of praxis as imperiled venture against established structures of meaning: a socio-ontological trajectory of human 'being' towards a transcendent horizon that is unstable, perpetually open and ever present at several removes from the Real.

For the Divine, as unforeseen opening, sublime possibility and inexhaustible horizon in correlation to existence, is dialectically unattainable. Therefore, seeking the Divine as insurmountable project[19] of human 'being' transcends the suffocating impasse and comprehensive materiality of the Real, as a daring seizure of implicated temporality and existential responsibility, actualizing dynamic metaphysical potentialities as 'no-thing-ness' towards an irresistible summons of 'presence-towards-self', an impossible lived rhythm of praxis enabling dense continuous lyrical flows of intentionality as contributions towards a more poetic constitution of human subjectivity.

For the human condition is such, that without search for, and recognition of, a transcendent horizon of meaning, lived experience can be rerouted

---

[19] "Thus the passion of man is the reverse of that of Christ, for man loses himself as man in order that God may be born. But the idea of God is contradictory and we lose ourselves in vain. Man is a useless passion." Sartre, p.784.

through biopolitical pacification and overdetermination-from-without into 'objecthood', and that rational animality which finds socio-ontological shelter
through unadulterated synchronicity with the bewildered herd. "To be shut up entirely to the past and
present is to the soul, whose life and happiness is
unceasing progress, what the prison is to the body –
a blight and a mildew, a hell of horrors."[20]

No doubt, the disaster of history mediates the
dialectic trajectory of human 'being' towards the
Divine that constitutes human subjectivity against
the Real. Human subjectivity is thus constituted by
lived rhythm of praxis as situated response of human 'being' to the call of history. "You have seen
how a man was made a slave; you shall see how a
slave was made a man."[21] Such an emancipatory
undertaking of radical ontological freedom thwarts
and disrupts attempts to embrace a spiritually de-
ceptive indulgence of metaphysical repose, 'fixed'
substantive identity and concrete stability, for it
necessarily involves a lived wager of implicated
temporality, full of uncertainty and without guarantee, thus entailing social risk, universal consequence
and total responsibility for 'being-in-the-world'.

---

[20] Frederick Douglass, *Life and Times of Frederick Douglass*,
(New York: Collier Books, 1892, 1962) p.156.
[21] Douglass, *Narrative of the Life of Frederick Douglass*, (New
Haven: Yale University Press, 1845, 2001) p.50.

This decisive open dialectic movement of situated consciousness towards the Divine, experienced as imperiled venture towards the world and intersubjective resonance towards one another, relentlessly transcends the Real through lived rhythm of praxis, or courts a myriad of socio-ontological dangers by falling prey to an overdetermination-from-without and biopolitical pacification that perpetually threaten to impose 'objecthood' upon the irreducibility of human agency and its irreconcilability with the Real.

the Raw of coloniality – Globally comprehensive constellations of racist dehumanization saturate lived
relations between western imperialist power and *the
wretched of the earth*[22] as coloniality. Empire sustains
coloniality through the normative gaze of modernity constituted by structural-inert violence and
miseducation of soul, as an unjust deterritorialized
topographical coherence that positions an imperial
mainstream superimposed over a socio-ontological
underground. This globalized consonance of established power justifies the persistence of that biopolitical signification of subhumanity called 'race', providing a rational anthropological basis for positing a
western imperialist continuum as the scientifically
evident journey of human evolution originating in a
blatant fetishization of nature, and ultimately culminating in modernity itself.

However, coloniality in the Raw discloses the presence of an irreducible socio-ontological intensity of
violence conceived during systematic endeavors of
overdetermination-from-without intent upon the
reduction of human 'being' to 'objecthood', as rationally cultivated and methodically undertaken dur-

---

[22] "the wretched of the earth are precisely the only people capable
of transforming life, and who change it every day towards
feeding, clothing and housing the whole of humanity." Sartre,
Critique of Dialectical Reason Vol.1, p.241. Modified translation
my own.

ing the biopolitical crucible of *chattel* slavery[23] that not only ushers in modernity, but serves as the very condition of its possibility.

The Raw of coloniality socio-ontologically permeates, although it is not synonymous with the hyperexploitation of labor by capital and the subsequent spiritual alienation and empirical commodification of human experience, as indicative of ever prevalent socio-historical relations within the imperial mainstream of modernity, which are even more pronounced in its current guise of advanced neo-liberal capitalist globalization. "What is termed globalization is the culmination of a process that began with the constitution of America and colonial/modern Euro-centered capitalism as new global powers. One of the fundamental axes of this model of power is the social classification of the world's population around the idea of race, a mental construction that expresses the basic experience of colonial domination and pervades the most important dimensions of global power, including its specific rationality: Eurocentrism. The racial axis has a colonial origin and character, but it has proven to be more durable

---

[23] "The first work of slavery is to mar and deface those characteristics of its victims which distinguish *men* from *things*, and *persons* from *property*. Its first aim is to destroy all sense of high moral and religious responsibility. It reduces man to a mere machine." Frederick Douglass, "The Nature of Slavery", *My Bondage and My Freedom*, (New York: Barnes & Noble Classics, 1850, 1855, 2005) pp.328-9.

and stable than the colonialism in whose matrix it was established. Therefore, the model of power that is globally hegemonic today presupposes an element of coloniality."[24]

Indeed, coloniality in the Raw implicates modernity as an ever-widening circumference of inscribed violence that binds structural-inert racist dehumanization to unprecedented cultural proliferations as passive social intermediations with the world, coercing human 'being' towards spiritual abdication of human subjectivity.

Coloniality in the Raw is thus located precisely in merciless proximity to the Real of a lived historical gravity binding western imperialist power and the Black Diaspora together as an imperial topographical coherence of biopolitical alterity. "This relation, in effect, as a *real antagonism*, is in no way reducible to the practico-inert ensemble of the process of exploitation: but it cannot be regarded as a genuine reciprocal praxis of struggle since it pits against one another series still paralyzed by alterity."[25] Such paralysis of alterity ensures a coerced absence of intersubjective resonance of human 'being' and social recognition amongst human community within Empire mediated by structural-inert violence as prefigured by the lived experience of

---

[24] Anibal Quijano, "Coloniality of Power, Eurocentrism and Latin America." *Coloniality At Large*, p.181
[25] Sartre, *Critique of Dialectical Reason Vol.1*, p.730.

"the African-American", who "suffers a more insuperable kind of subjugation than would be true under pure colonialism: he cannot sever his ties with his rulers and go his own way." [26]

And yet, as the Douglassian anti-slavery dialectic[27] suggests, emancipatory praxis initiates irreconcilable historical momentum towards transforming an exceptional antagonism into an exceptional antagonistic reciprocity, thus overcoming the socio-ontological paralysis of biopolitical alterity, enabling potentialities for an insurgent geonational trajectory of unremitting confrontation with western imperialist power, even while simultaneously coexisting in unrelentingly close and indivisible geoterritorial proximity.

---

[26] Harold Cruse, *Rebellion or Revolution*, (New York: Apollo Editions, 1968) p.70.
[27] Douglass, *Life and Times of Frederick Douglass*, pp.134-144.

postmodern lumpenproletariat (double or nothing) –
Postmodern lumpenproletariat consciousness draws strength and sustenance from the biopolitically
dangerous assertion of human 'being' associated
with those condemned by a western imperialist continuum to wander the anthropological wastelands
of 'race' and suffer the Raw of coloniality as the
socio-ontological underground of modernity. For is
not the very mention and classification of *under*privileged, *under*developed, *under*educated, *under*employed and *under*represented populations of toiling
masses, indicative of a globalized *under*class that
discloses oppressive historical conditions which
contribute towards a lived ontological positionality
that confers a generalized social withdrawal of basic
human consideration under the normative gaze of
Empire?

As such, it would be a mistake to assign the postmodern lumpenproletariat a permanent categorical
rigidity as nominally associated with vulgar class or
essential 'race' specific determinism. Look around,
or better yet, gaze forward at the approaching horizon of geohistorical momentum. Right here amongst persecuted populations and exploited immigrants, and even over there amidst internment camps
of postnational refugees. Globally displaced, racially outcast, mainstream heretics, spiritual outsiders,
existential outlaws, historically marginalized, socio-
ontologically illicit and yet ultimately burdened

with geonational significance: *the wretched of the earth*.

As socio-ontological fugitives arising from the underground of modernity and perpetual exiles awakening from the vain stupor of the imperial mainstream, both share creative potentialities of human agency and an intersubjective resonance of solidarity from which to socially constitute an insurgent working unity through diversity between the 'grassroots' who revolt in existential proximity to the Real of oppression itself, and the 'elites' who rebel based on epistemological proximity to the Real about such ongoing oppression. What unites 'grassroots' and 'elites' as a postmodern lumpen-proletariat is not some 'fixed' materialist causality, but a metaphysical Truth of kinship and radical venture of emancipatory praxis originating in the global magnitude of an undifferentiated choice of geonational *insurrection-for-itself* against Empire.

lived coherence of imperial topography – Empire recognizes no horizontal limitations, thus deterritorializing coloniality through structural-inert reconfigurations of a western imperialist continuum as topographically coherent lived relations of power between an imperial mainstream of modernity and socio-ontological underground.

Indeed, even when geohistorical proximity between underground and mainstream positionality increases, the Raw of coloniality exhibits a lived persistence, exacerbating the intersubjective resonance and intermediations of human 'being-in-the-world'. "What white Americans have never fully understood – but what the Negro can never forget – is that white society is deeply implicated in the ghetto. White institutions created it, white institutions maintain it, and white society condones it."[28]

And yet, by its steady encroachment of what was formerly outside, Empire accounts for gaping geohistorical wounds of coloniality as a coextensive socio-cultural integration of biopolitical alterity in lived topographical coherence to the normative gaze; thus ultimately globally consolidating a paradigm of oppression that is intimately familiar to Black community throughout the Diaspora. "Imperial sovereignty means that no point of space or

---

[28] *Report of the National Advisory Commission on Civil Disorders*, (New York: Bantam Books, 1968) p.2.

time and no element of biopolitical tissue is safe from intervention. The electronic archiving of the world, generalized traceability, the fact that the means of production are becoming just as much a means of control, the reduction of the juridical edifice to a mere weapon in the arsenal of the norm – all this tends to turn everyone into *a suspect*."[29]

As such, the continuity of the imperial mainstream's murderous universality as simulation of the human condition "no longer needs to be rational, because it no longer measures itself against either an ideal or negative instance. It is no longer anything but operational";[30] therefore ensuring a coercive anonymity under which Black subjectivity-as-human 'being' quietly disappears without incident.

---

[29] Tiqqun, *Introduction to Civil War*, (Los Angeles: Semiotext(e), 2010) p.157.
[30] Jean Baudrillard, *The Perfect Crime*, (London: Verso, 1999) p.5.

exceptional antagonism of ascendant humanity – The global hegemony of Empire constitutes an exceptional situation of 'being-in-the-world' against which we experience the irreducibility of our human agency and its irreconcilability with the Real as radical ontological freedom of the human condition.

Indeed, the rational signification of subhumanity designated as 'race' ideologically colludes with a history of massive global importation, exportation and enslavement of human 'being', rounding up people, families, communities by the masses – murdering, displacing, imprisoning, raping, beating, branding and torturing human 'being' into a functional subservience of 'objecthood'. This violent biopolitical crucible of *chattel* slavery as coloniality in the Raw, positions vast populations of human 'being' as the socio-ontological underground of modernity[31] – subhuman foils to a mainstream pop-

---

[31] "Modern imperialism and modern industrialism are one and the same system; root and branch of the same tree. The race problem is the *other side* of labor problem; . . . remembering always that *empire* is the heavy hand of capital abroad . . . this almost naïve setting of the darker races beyond the pale of democracy and of modern humanity . . . involves two things – acquiescence of the darker peoples and agreement between capital and labor in white democracies." W.E.B. DuBois, "The Negro Mind Reaches Out", included in *The New Negro*, edited by Alain Locke, (New York: Touchstone Book, 1925, 1992) p.386 & 402. Emphasis mine. "From the beginning, the American Negro has existed as a colonial being. His enslavement coincided with the colonial expansion of European powers and was nothing more or less than

ulated, sanitized and organized according to the normative gaze of a western imperialist continuum.

"In a normalizing society, race or racism is the precondition that makes killing acceptable. . . . When I say 'killing,' I obviously do not mean simply murder as such, but also every form of indirect murder; the fact of exposing someone to death, increasing the risk of death for some people, or, quite simply, political death, expulsion, rejection, and so on."[32] 'Race' thus serves as an anthropological conduit for a perpetual reception of objective violence that subsidizes means of production and modes of exploitation towards generating ceaseless labor, spearheading vast accumulations of capital facilitating the flourishing of systematic global trade towards configuring and reconfiguring structural-inert foundations for the socio-historical triumph of modernity itself.

Therefore, genuine assertion of Black subjectivity-as-human 'being' constitutes a 'problem'[33] and 'bio-political danger'[34] that introduces an ascendant rupture at the anthropological core of modernity, disclosing a greater socio-ontological range of the

a condition of domestic colonialism." Cruse, *Rebellion or Revolution*, p.76.
[32] Michel Foucault, *"Society Must Be Defended"*, (New York: Picador, 1976, 2003) p.256
[33] DuBois, *The Souls of Black Folk*, p.1-7.
[34] Fanon, *Black Skin, White Masks*, p.161-5. Foucault, pp.254-8.

human condition, and hence simultaneously revealing more variable atmospheres of emancipatory
praxis than can possibly be exhausted by vulgar
unmediated loyalty to any loud mechanistic deities
of biological determinism. False deities which lead
us further along an arid epistemological labyrinth of
materialist causality that somehow always culmin-
ates in that all too familiar and comfortable *cul de
sac* of an 'end of history' populated by unrepentant
clones of western bourgeois subjectivity within an
exact reproduction of a western imperialist continuum.

No reconciliation is possible between the everyday strivings of an ascendant humanity asserting
Black subjectivity-as-human 'being' and contemporary reconfigurations of western imperialist power
that inscribe the original violent biopolitical reduction of human 'being' to 'objecthood' through *chattel*
slavery, into a sovereign legitimacy of Empire.

This structural-inert violence, which is inscribed
in modernity as passive socio-cultural mediations,
necessitates its own reconstitution into blatant violent praxis whenever confronted by human agency
originating from Black subjectivity. This is how neo-
colonial police agents, overcome with an alarming
sense of 'biopolitical danger', drive a squad car onto
a snowy playground in Cleveland, Ohio, open fire

and murder 12-year-old Tamir Rice[35] who was harmlessly playing by himself with a toy gun, and how a seemingly routine traffic stop for a supposedly improper turn signal translates into Sandra Bland[36], eyes wide open, dead in a Texas jail cell. Indeed, the socio-ontologically stifling systematic rigor of globalized racist dehumanization is in itself a stirring testament to the very force of ascendant humanity being subjugated.

Maintaining the topographic anthropological hierarchy of modernity, which consists of an imperial mainstream populated by Man-as-western bourgeois subjectivity, and a socio-ontological underground overpopulated by *the wretched of the earth*, necessitates a constant renewal of that constitutive primacy of unaccountable violence against Black subjectivity-as-human 'being', thereby rendering such violence structural-inert ie. objective in scope and rational in application.[37]

Thus neo-colonial police agents function in accordance with the normative gaze of established power; whether beating Rodney King down to a

---

[35] Krishnadev Calamur, "No Indictment in the Tamir Rice Shooting", *The Atlantic* (theatlantic.com) December 28, 2015.
[36] Molly Hennessy-Fiske, "Texas Grand Jury Finds No Cause for Indictment in Sandra Bland Case", *Los Angeles Times* (latimes.com) December 21, 2015.
[37] "the objective violence which defines the system itself as a practico-inert hell." Jean-Paul Sartre, *Critique of Dialectical Reason Vol.1*, p.718.

writhing disfigured mass of blood and flesh in Los Angeles, California; or murdering Tyron Lewis in St. Petersburg, Florida; or murdering Timothy Thomas in Cincinnati, Ohio; or 'accidentally' electrocuting Zyed Benna and Bouna Traore to death in the suburbs of Paris, France; or murdering Mark Duggan in Tottenham, North London, England; or putting a bullet in the back of Oscar Grant while he was lying face down with his hands around his back in Oakland, California; or murdering Kimani Gray in Brooklyn, New York; or murdering Michael Brown with his hands raised to the sky in Ferguson, Missouri; or 'accidentally' breaking the spinal cord and thereby killing Freddie Gray in Baltimore, Maryland, they are merely operating with whatever reasonable force is required to pacify the insurgent trajectory of an ascendant humanity by "murdering men wherever they find them, at the corner of every one of their own streets, in all the corners of the globe."[38]

And yet, by each one of these 'racial incidents' disclosing a lived persistence of coloniality in the Raw, historical openings towards galvanizing the Return of oppressive violence back to source as insurrection-in-itself against Empire become manifest and even more socially accessible.

---

[38] Frantz Fanon, *The Wretched of the Earth*, p.311.

As such, any radical shift of philosophical interrogation and epistemological orientation which existentially recognizes the irreducible human 'being' of lived Black experience, reveals an exceptional antagonism[39] that introduces inevitable tremors of geohistorical disequilibrium along socio-ontological fault lines of racist dehumanization and coloniality in the Raw, which undergird the global foundations of modernity itself.

---

[39] "For Black people, civic stability is a state of emergency." Frank B. Wilderson III, *Red, White & Black: Cinema and the Structure of U.S. Antagonisms*, (Durham: Duke University Press, 2010) p.79. And yet, Wilderson's Afropessimist orientation elaborates a fixed identity and structural positionality of Blackness towards an accurate grammar of suffering, whereas existential liberation theory enunciates an insurgent trajectory of lived Black experience towards emancipatory praxis. Therefore, this exceptional antagonism existing between the normative gaze of a western imperialist continuum and the assertion of Black subjectivity-as-human 'being' is often misread within the normative gaze itself by Afropessimist thought as an ontological antagonism between "the Human" and "Blackness". This misreading runs the risk of exhausting any emancipatory potentialities of human agency towards resistance, by ceding constitutive authority towards determining what it means to be human to the normative gaze of Empire.

'being' and insurrection – Ascendant humanity remains defenseless against the structural-inert violence
of established power only to the degree to which we
cede the scope of our existential responsibility and
dismiss the irreducibility of our human agency. For
no matter the consequence, all modes of resistance
against injustice and oppression begin with a decision of irreducible agency as commitment to a trajectory of emancipatory praxis, thus initiating lived
potentialities for the cultivation of human subjectivity from which to continually manifest ever more
dynamic realizations of human liberation.

Even in the face of overwhelming odds as maintained through an unaccountable violence constituted by neo-colonial police towards renewing the
sovereign legitimacy of Empire, the rebellion of
even one human 'being' implicates ascendant humanity with potentialities of intersubjective resonance
from which to either accept or reject the normative
gaze of a western imperialist continuum. Hence a
horizon of possibility manifests from which we
decide to get in groove with that socio-ontological
rhythm of constitutive self-determination, relentless
transcendence and spiritual upheaval which discloses the human condition as situated consciousness.

In the midst of insurrection-in-itself as an ongoing
dynamic of protest-as-resistance and spontaneous
rebellion, an ominous moving wall of neo-colonial

police in full riot gear amasses before a loose formation of Black youth-as-ascendant humanity in Baltimore, Maryland. An immediacy of dread conditions the intersubjective resonance of these youth towards uniting against the Raw coloniality of an approaching confrontation with structural-inert violence embodied in police agents.

And yet, as dread distinguishes itself from fear by heralding the possibility of emancipatory praxis against the tidal inevitability of imperial repression, an uninhibited rediscovery of human agency against the Real of a pervasive biopolitical pacification of Black community achieves realization in the decision of one brother to pick up a rock, throw it at the neo-colonial police and initiate a Return of structural-inert violence back to source. This compelling rediscovery of human agency floods lived Black experience with a vertigo of emancipatory praxis against the dread of biopolitical persecution, disrupting the concrete stability of the Real as tremors of history begin to accelerate against the imperial coherence of a world seismically shifting unpredictably and moving spontaneously from underneath.

Invariably, another brother picks up a rock in solidarity and joins the melee by launching a throw. Then another brother chooses to do so, and then yet another, as well as a sister. Each brother, and each sister, enacts 'being-for-one another' through an intermediary gaze, by which they see one another resisting, as each constitutes such resistance as themselves in Revolt. The decision to resist, in itself constitutes a lived unity as 'being-for-one another' through mutually recognizing the social trajectory and ontological implications of each brother's, and each sister's, resistance as their own. As such, each act of resistance simultaneously binds their kinetic distance of interiority with an intersubjective resonance as a lived unity in renunciation of the sovereign legitimacy of western imperialist power and spiritual affirmation of their shared and inviolable human 'being'.

As each decision towards asserting Black subjectivity-as-human 'being' contributes a rhythmic acceleration increasing the dialectic tempo as intersubjective resonance of Revolt amongst them, the antagonistic reciprocity realized by their emancipatory praxis manifests itself through the sheer socio-ontological momentum of resistance that tangibly halts the explicit gravitational impetus of neocolonial police repression before the intermediary gaze of the world, and pushes back against the barricades of sovereign legitimacy meant to isolate Black liberation within the veil of symbolic victory and hence at a safe distance from engaging history.

As such, what begins as an insufficient act of resistance by one brother becomes an ontological point of departure, which raises the social threshold as spiritual unity for all of those present to existentially overcome the geohistorical limitations enforced against the intersubjective resonance of human solidarity by the violent aggression of neo-colonial police. For as each brother, and each sister, hurls Davidian projectiles at the Goliath of oppression, the simulacrum of 'protest-as-ritual event' dissipates, unable to sustain the weight of historical significance introduced by an exceptional antagonistic reciprocity which discloses ever new horizons of emancipatory potentialities in affirmation of authentic human subjectivity-as-lived universal through simultaneous renunciation of the normative gaze of a western imperialist continuum.

Hence the intersubjective resonance of Revolt embodied in these Black youth encounters the precipice of anomie, not as a one-way street or *cul de sac*, but as a lived acclivity and declivity of ethical and legal indeterminacy which structures existing relations of socio-ontological positionality between sovereign legitimacy of western imperialist power and exceptional antagonism of lived Black experience.[40] For the socio-onotological positionality of

---

[40] "Modern sovereignties harbor a blind spot, a zone in which power is above the law and thus, at least potentially, a terrain of

lived Black experience asymmetrically undercuts the juridical structure and maintenance of the imperial mainstream-as-civil society.

No doubt, even relevant concerns regarding the steady encroachment of totalitarian security culture upon the liberal democratic prestige of the imperial mainstream, risk veiling the Raw of coloniality that already exists between western imperialist power and *the wretched of the earth,* and thus render obsolete the racist dehumanization that substantiates the juridical scope of 'liberal democracy'. "But if the existence of violence outside the law, as pure immediate violence, is assured, this furnishes proof that revolutionary violence, the highest manifestation of unalloyed violence by man, is possible, and shows by what means."[41] Therefore, in resisting the accumulative slaughter of human 'being' by neo-colonial police via this biopolitical threshold of indeterminacy, the trajectory of emancipatory praxis confronts an imposition of struc-

---

terror. This wild zone of power, by its very structure impossible to domesticate, is intrinsic to mass-democratic regimes. It makes no difference whether the model of their legitimacy is the liberal claim of political (formal) democracy based on universal, mass suffrage, or the socialist claim of economic (substantive) democracy based on egalitarian distribution of social goods." Susan Buck-Morss, *Dreamworld and Catastrophe*, (Cambridge: MIT Press, 2000) pp.2-3.

[41] Walter Benjamin, *Selected Writings Vol.1 1913-1926*, (Cambridge: Belknap/Harvard University Press, 1996, 2004) p.252.

tural-inert violence without legitimate form that incessantly legitimates and reconfigures the topographical coherence of Empire.[42]

As such, emancipatory praxis unsettles the coercive anonymity of structural-inert violence, and therefore reignites an originary confrontation of exceptional antagonistic reciprocity which calls into question the sovereign legitimacy of a western imperialist continuum. Indeed, "how do we pass from an atmosphere of violence to violence in action?"[43]

The ensuing confrontation between a rebirth of genuine human subjectivity-as-lived universal and the tyranny of established unjust global power, inaugurates *insurrection-in-itself* as yet another socio-historical phenomenon towards making geo-national *insurrection-for-itself* possible . . .

---

[42] "the state of exception is neither external nor internal to the juridical order, and the problem of defining it concerns precisely a threshold, or a zone of indifference, where inside and outside do not exclude each other but rather blur with each other. The suspension of the norm does not mean its abolition, and the zone of anomie that it establishes is not (or at least claims not to be) unrelated to the juridical order." Giorgio Agamben, *State of Exception*, (Chicago: University of Chicago Press, 2003, 2005) p.23.

[43] Fanon, *The Wretched of the Earth*, p.71.

vertigo of emancipatory praxis – In the immediate aftermath of *insurrection-in-itself* in Baltimore, Maryland, the evidence of a contravening movement against the systemic deodorization of the murder of Man lingers as the residue of tear gas mixes with a potent scent of kerosene, waste cotton and motor oil induced smoke and flames.

As such, Revolt renders the socio-ontological disaster of modernity discernible by the proliferation of such stench accompanying a temporary landscape of imperial discontinuity littered with the debris of history and shattered glass, amidst shadows of burnt-out edifices and overturned neo-colonial police vehicles charred by the fires of spontaneous rebellion and protest-as-resistance. Closer observation of these conquered war machines of occupying power, reveals the indelible markings of having been assailed and stomped out in force by the workboots and sneakers of an ascendant humanity.

Indeed, the assertion of Black subjectivity-as-human 'being' within modernity as imposed by a western imperialist continuum, discloses dread as situated consciousness interrogating potentialities of human agency through confrontation against a comprehensive ambiguity of existence inebriated with the historical inevitability of socio-ontological persecution as biopolitical pacification and over-determination-from-without.

Choosing to confront this dread with emancipatory praxis induces the conditions of possibility for vertigo within lived Black experience. However, this vertigo of emancipatory praxis is not limited to Wilderson's conception of "subjective vertigo" as "a dizzying sense that one is moving or spinning in an otherwise stationary world", nor is it exhausted by positing "objective vertigo" as "the sensation that one is not simply spinning in an otherwise stable environment," but "that one's environment is perpetually unhinged". For rather than resulting from "a life constituted by disorientation" or "a life interrupted by disorientation", the vertigo of emancipatory praxis vividly informs *a life that disorients* established structures of meaning.[44]

That is, a vertigo indicative of an inebriating socio-ontological dynamic that accompanies constitutive self-determination as it introduces disorienttation within the normative gaze by the assertion of Black subjectivity-as-human 'being'. As such, are there any ramparts of historical certitude from which to buttress the Real or justify established

---

[44] Frank B. Wilderson III, "The Vengeance of Vertigo: Aphasia and Abjection in the Political Trials of Black Insurgents", *Intensions*, Issue#5.0, Fall/Winter 2011. See also *The Brotherwise Dispatch*, Vol.2, Issue#8, June-August/2013.

structures of meaning without first presupposing a geohistorical imperative of Revolt against Empire?

Vertigo, as consciousness accelerating in dialectic tempo towards unsettling existential paradigms of absolute certitude, simultaneously reorients rhythms of socio-ontological bearing against any derivations of 'fixed' identity originating from a harmonious acclimation to the normative gaze.

And yet, by disrupting the topography of imperial coherence that characterizes established structures of meaning, vertigo introduces a severity of spiritual disorientation within the normative gaze as a necessary correlate of emancipatory praxis which torrentially mediates and contests the Real. "We are forever pursued by our actions. Their ordering, their circumstances, and their motivation may perfectly well come to be profoundly modified *a postereori*. This is merely one of the snares history and its various influences sets for us. But can we escape being dizzy? And who can affirm that vertigo does not haunt the whole of existence?"[45] Against its reductionist metaphysical appropriation by a neuropsychological determinism, vertigo as inebriating movement of situated consciousness realizes itself as an adrenaline rush of emancipatory praxis overcoming dread.

---

[45] Frantz Fanon, *The Wretched of the Earth*, p.253.

transcendent beauty of presence – The mythology of a 'fixed', 'stable' and 'empirical self', that commands a strange and unreflective fealty, merely veils the naked interiority and transcendent beauty of kinetic distance the human condition experiences as an unforgiving 'presence-towards-self' from which to constitute human subjectivity against the Real of hegemonic structures of meaning endorsed by Empire.

The concrete 'empirical self', birthed through an epistemological divorce that desituates consciousness from lived experience as an exercise in the futile preservation of Man-as-western bourgeois subjectivity, reeks with the stench of accumulative slaughter of human 'being' littered throughout modernity. The geohistorical murder of Man stains consciousness with the sedentary blood of Bad Faith[46] as self-deception, spiritual evasion and ontological repose. This socio-ontological disaster enables and aids that offbeat hubris of biological determinism in interrupting the coarse vitality and minimalist rhythm of constitutive self-determination, relentless transcendence and spiritual upheaval that distinguishes ascendant humanity from rational animality.

---

[46] Jean-Paul Sartre, *Being and Nothingness*, pp.86-116. Lewis R. Gordon, *Bad Faith and Anti-Black Racism*, (Amherst, New York: Humanity Press, 1995, 1999).

keepin' it hyperreal n*gga!? – When the normative gaze issues forth blatant ideological pronouncements suggesting the inevitable murder of the Real, it is not out of any rational expectation of success associated with such a daunting task, but rather for the unmitigated cultivation of Spectacle which unfolds through the funeral of its corresponding sign.

As such, "this is the story of a crime – the murder of reality. . . But the fact is that the crime is never perfect, for the world betrays itself by appearances . . ."[47] The word 'nigger', as the sign of a deliberate materialist grafting of 'objecthood' on human 'being' in semiotic correspondence with the Real of racist dehumanization that permeates modernity, has been declared dead and buried by the Black wing of the hyperbourgeoisie through the integrated institutional auspices of an actual 'funeral' hosted by the NAACP.[48] Through this self-congratulatory 'abolishing' of the word 'nigger', the normative gaze begins a process of detaching the Real from its correspondence with the sign towards a coercive ontological anonymity which assists a global hegemony of advanced neo-liberal capitalism to render the socio-historical domination of Black people into a more complete and even banal oppression.

---

[47] Baudrillard, *The Perfect Crime*, p.1.
[48] *Associated Press*, Monday July 9th, 2007.

Already superbly acclimated to the monotony of structural-inert oppression as experienced in an advanced neo-liberal capitalist society and in self-serving complicity with established power, the Black hyperbourgeosie, whose assimilationist ideology "is meant to further their own class aims, and the aspirations of the masses only incidentally";[49] are engaged in carrying out a postracial discursive cultural makeover of the foundational socio-historical specificities of racist dehumanization which inform modernity. This is done by translating genuine righteous outrage at the racist dehumanization of Black people into an urgent concern for siphoning away the intensity of potent unsanctioned language and semiotic orientations which still manage to disclose the Real of our persisting subjugation to a western imperialist continuum.

This epistemological parlor trick, by reducing all forms of rational concern about the racist oppression of human 'being' to a matter of mere linguistic triviality, meant to solely address and assuage our emotional well-being, creates a simulation which circumvents actual confrontation of injustice when engaging in social discourse, specifically whenever

---

[49] Cruse, *Rebellion or Revolution*, p.59. Cruse continues on, ". . . the Afro American middle class knows little of culture, art, politics and world events, so involved is it in seeking personal status as close as possible to the middle-class white world and its values." p.61.

said injustice discursively manifests itself in 'racial' tones. This has the much desired ideological effect of promoting a gnawing critical silence regarding the actual phenomenon of racist injustice against human 'being' as a standard of legitimacy in public opinion.

The word 'nigger' is an insult. Yet this insult, this word, this symbol, has no causal relation to the structural-inert oppression of Black people by a western imperialist continuum. It is a word which is insulting because it is meant to remind us of a forced socio-ontological subjugation of human 'being' to an overwhelming geohistorical violence which, although constantly transitioning between poles of legitimacy and illegitimacy, remains as an unceasingly 'objective' constant of lived Black experience accompanying the onset of modernity.

The word 'nigger' is a semiotic remnant of a singularly 'fixed' severity of lived 'objecthood' imposed upon human 'being' through the crucible of *chattel* slavery.[50] The very vulgarity of the word

---

[50] "Slavery in the United States is the granting of that power by which one man exercises and enforces a right of property on the body and soul of another. The condition of a slave is simply that of a brute beast. He is a piece of property – a marketable commodity, in the language of the law, to be bought and sold at the will and caprice of the master who claims him to be his property; he is spoken of, thought of, and treated as property." Frederick Douglass, *Autobiographies*, (New York: Library of America, 1845, 1855, 1881, 1994) p.400.

itself discursively reaffirms that epistemological consolidation of subhumanity called 'race', which veils the irreducible agency of constitutive self-determination, relentless transcendence and spiritual upheaval that characterizes the human condition. This much maligned word 'nigger', however, cannot be completely grasped without understanding its much more respectable version, 'negro'.

As Wright reminds us, the "word 'Negro,' the term by which, orally or in print, we black folk in the United States are usually designated, is not really a name at all nor a description, but a psychological island whose objective form is the most unanimous fiat in all American history; a fiat buttressed by popular and national tradition, and written down in many state and city statutes, a fiat which artificially and arbitrarily defines, regulates, and limits in scope of meaning the vital contours of our lives, and the lives of our children and our children's children." [51]

---

[51] Wright continues on, "This island, within whose confines we live, is anchored in the feelings of millions of people, and is situated in the midst of the sea of white faces we meet each day; and, by and large, as three hundred years of time has borne our nation into the twentieth century, its rocky boundaries have remained unyielding to the waves of our hope that dash against it.

The steep cliffs of this island are manifest, on the whole, in the conduct of whites toward us hour by hour, a conduct which tells us that we possess no rights commanding respect, that we have no claim to pursue happiness in our own fashion, that our progress toward civilization constitutes an insult, that our behavior must be

To be a 'nigger' or a 'negro' are exactly the same, in that they both signify being "sealed" into a "crushing objecthood". "'Dirty nigger!' or simply, 'Look, a Negro!' I came into the world imbued with the will to find a meaning in things, my spirit filled with a desire to attain the source of the world and then I found that I was an object in the midst of other objects."[52] And yet in general social discourse the word 'negro' is significantly less controversial and regarded as nowhere near as vulgar or offensive a term as 'nigger'.

This is indicative of the normative gaze of a western imperialist continuum, which at its core, maintains and legitimizes the anthropological distinction between Black subjectivity and human 'being' within an epistemology of sanctioned essentialist discourse on 'race', while at the same time allowing Black people to experience a socially controlled and self-gratifying marginal liberalism which comes from much applauded efforts to condemn any unofficial, illegitimate crude variants of the exact same sign of 'racist' dehumanization.

kept firmly within an orbit branded as inferior, that we must be compelled to labor at the behest of others, that as a group we are owned by the whites, and that manliness on our part warrants instant reprisal." Richard Wright, *12 Million Black Voices* included in *Richard Wright Reader*, edited by Ellen Wright & Michael Fabre, (New York: Da Capo Press, 1941, 1997) pp.160-1.

[52] Fanon, *Black Skin, White Masks*, p.109.

That both terms 'negro' and 'nigger' originate from the same western imperialist continuum is stridently and consciously overlooked as a gratuitous and reformist demonstration of goodwill by those who seek to curry favor with established power. It would appear that the best place to hide key semiotic indicators of violently imposed Black subhumanity is actually in the plain sight of social legitimacy. Indeed, "the genealogy of racism in the West is inseparable from the classificatory category of race in natural history."[53]

In this regard, the work of Locke and DuBois during the Harlem Renaissance is of vital theoretical significance due to their profound influence upon a dialectical turn in the ongoing discourse of Black liberation towards socio-historical recognition and ontological reconstitution of Black subjectivity-as-human 'being'. For it is in the discourse and debates surrounding the 'New Negro' arising from the intersubjective resonance of Black community in the immediate post-World War I era that a renewal of that universal historical imperative of social unrest towards Black liberation in confrontation with western imperialist power is disclosed.[54] This

---

[53] West, *Prophesy Deliverance!*, p.55.
[54] For an excellent collection of primary sources containing the discursive controversies and intellectual melees of that era involving A. Phillip Randolph, Marcus Garvey, W.E.B. DuBois, Cyril V. Briggs, Chandler Owen, Alain Locke, etc., see *Voices of*

'New Negro' reconstitution of Black subjectivity encompasses a lived tension of awakening class consciousness, political agitation and cultural nationalism that ultimately finds its foremost discursive articulation within an emancipatory aesthetics of cultural pluralism. "The mind of the Negro seems suddenly to have slipped from under the tyranny of social intimidation and to be shaking off the psychology of imitation and implied inferiority. By shedding the old chrysalis of the Negro problem we are achieving something like a spiritual emancipation."[55]

Precisely by "shedding the old chrysalis of the Negro problem", Locke pushes beyond previous socio-ontological boundaries which centered around a pragmatic assimilationist "psychology of imitation" that merely reconstituted western bourgeois standards within a Black subjectivity thoroughly wedded to American nationalist chauvinism out of genuine concern for basic human survival. As such, "achieving" this "spiritual emancipation" by the Lockean 'New Negro' ultimately confronts modernity with refreshingly new aesthetic potentialities that disrupt the normative gaze. "Subtly the conditions that are molding a New Negro are also

a Black Nation: Political Journalism in the Harlem Renaissance, edited by Theodore Vincent, (Trenton: Africa World Press, 1973).
[55] Alain Locke, *The New Negro: Voices of the Harlem Renaissance*, p.4.

molding a new American attitude."[56]   Thus the Harlem Renaissance can be understood as a Muhammad Ali 'rope-a-dope' strategy of cultural pluralist pugilism against the imperial mainstream-as-civil society.   During which, Black community engaged in a survivalist assimilation of western bourgeois standards that functionally cut off the boxing ring of historical movement towards authentic universality by accepting social limitations as tantamount to receiving a beat down in the early rounds of modernity while cornered against the ropes of a perpetual 'objecthood'.   However, at times between rounds, and sometimes late in rounds right before the bell, almost as if to remind established power of the indomitable spiritual depths of the human condition, emancipatory aesthetics originating in the disaster of lived Black experience unleashed flurries of cultural resistance as the Blues metaphysic took advantage of lapses in hegemonic stamina and epistemological weariness to land a few well-placed discursive combinations to the normative gaze, timed with a pugilistic precision to take advantage whenever the imperial mainstream-as-civil society ideologically over-extended itself, as exemplified in the post-World War I era.

Even that almighty deity of American nationalist exceptionalism suffered a significant loss of

---

[56] Locke, p.10.

prestige by simultaneously urging an all-out war against global injustice abroad while dissuading armed confrontation with local injustice at home. As such, the normative gaze found itself on the receiving end of cultural resistance as swift combinations of overhand rights and left jabs by an aesthetic rebellion of Black subjectivity introduced disequilibrium within the coloniality of topographical coherence that binds imperial mainstream-as-civil society to the socio-ontological underground of modernity. "What do we want? What is the thing we are after? As it was phrased last night it had a certain truth: We want to be Americans, full-fledged Americans, with all the rights of other American citizens. But is that all? Do we simply want to be Americans? Once in a while through all of us there flashes some clairvoyance, some clear idea, of what America really is. We who are dark can see America in a way white Americans cannot. And seeing our country thus, are we satisfied with its present goals and ideals?"[57]

The Harlem Renaissance furthered an ongoing confrontation with modernity by an ascendant humanity engaged in aesthetic-ontological rebellion, fueled by the tension of an exceptional antagonism between the assertion of Black subjectivity-as-hum-

---

[57] W.E.B. DuBois, "Criteria of Negro Art", *The Crisis Magazine*, October 1926.

an 'being' and a western imperialist continuum. Paradoxically, fighting for an American armed forces which preserved and strengthened western imperialist power on a global scale during World War I, drastically heightened the radical potentialities for armed struggle and resistance against western imperialist power as it manifest itself locally in racist tyranny and injustice within the context of the American nation-state. DuBois understood this even more clearly than Locke: "Under similar circumstances, we would fight again. But by the God of Heaven, we are cowards and jackasses if now that the war is over, we do not marshal every ounce of our brain and brawn to fight a sterner, longer, more unbending battle against the forces of Hell in our own land. We return. We return from fighting. We return fighting."[58]

However, as these emancipatory potentialities began bearing fruit in the lived experience of Black people, an unadulterated ritual savagery of lynching as organized grassroots biopolitical mob violence, already a murderous historical constant of our 'being-in-the-world', was even further unleashed upon Black community and grew fiercer in direct proportion to everyday assertions of freedom as an ascendant humanity. This climaxed in the pervasive suppression and bloody struggle for

---

[58] DuBois, "Returning Soldiers", *The Crisis Magazine*, May 1919.

Stover |81

human liberation as exemplified during, but in no ways limited to, that infamous Red summer of 1919, which set the tone for the Harlem Renaissance that followed in its wake as a socio-ontological confrontation of the false sedentary universality of Man-as-western bourgeois subjectivity through Black aesthetic revolt and cultural affirmation of human 'being'.

With soldiers returning from direct military involvement on behalf of the American nation-state during World War I, Black people once again placed tremendous expectations of human solidarity upon an American populace still in ignorant refusal, or informed denial, of our shared humanity. And much like the aftermath of the Revolutionary War and the Civil War, these historical expectations were betrayed by both ruling power elite and toiling American masses under a united front of 'white' identity that actually continues to socially neutralize the supposed revolutionary political determinism of antagonistic economic class interests. "And while Negro labor in America suffers because of the fundamental inequities of the whole capitalistic system, the lowest and most fatal degree of its suffering comes not from the capitalists but from fellow white laborers."[59]

---

[59] DuBois continues on "It is not a sufficient answer to say that capital encourages this oppression and uses it for its own ends.

The proletariat, who are relied on by the capitalist ruling power elite to enforce and legitimize western imperialist power by dogmatic adherence to the biopolitically constructed fiction of 'race', are also simultaneously counted upon by Marxist revolutionary theory to act as an emancipatory force of geohistorical importance because of some mythic revolutionary determinism inherent in economic class identity. Whereas the prelude to World War I saw the working class betray its own revolutionary internationalist rhetoric and orientation, the aftermath of World War I saw this petty 'wonderbread' cultural nationalist working class resume the murder of Man; as brutal bewildered herds of rational animality ritually accosted men like William Little who was actually lynched for not taking off his United States Army uniform.[60]

This may have excused the ignorant and superstitious Russian peasants in the past and some of the poor whites of the South today. But the bulk of white labor is neither ignorant nor fanatical. It knows exactly what it is doing and means to do it. William Green and Matthew Wolf of the A.F. of L. have no excuse of illiteracy to veil their deliberate intention to keep Negroes and Mexicans and other elements of common labor, in a lower proletariat as subservient to their interests as theirs are to the interests of capital." DuBois, "Marxism and the Negro Problem", *The Crisis Magazine*, May 1933.

[60] Ralph Ginzburg, *100 Years of Lynchings*, (Baltimore: Black Classic Press, 1962, 1988) p.118.

As such, the Harlem Renaissance was justifiably "radical in tone yet not in purpose",[61] for this 'New Negro' subjectivity challenged then prevailing Marxist dogma which made no allowances for the possibility of any other legitimate revolutionary subjectivity outside the 'white-as-universal' working class. That much needed anthropological revaluation and epistemological 'stretching' of Marxist categories initiated by DuBoisian critical theory and so integral to the existential liberationist orientation of Fanon and Sartre was now underway.[62]

Black subjectivity-as-ascendant humanity arises from beneath normative anthropological standards of modernity, drawing its radical emancipatory imperative at swords edge of human 'being' lived as constant tension of socio-ontological alterity subjugated by a western imperialist continuum. However, the historical aftershocks unleashed from such an unprecedented seismic epistemological shift would gradually register over time with ever growing intersubjective resonance. For it would not be until future generations truly reaped an emancipatory harvest from the socio-ontological seeds of aesthetic rebellion implicit in the Harlem Renaissance, that this dialectic wager by Locke and DuBois could even be truly appreciated and under-

---

[61] Locke, *The New Negro*, p.11.
[62] Fanon, *The Wretched of the Earth* and Sartre, *Critique of Dialectical Reason Vol.1.*

stood. "We black folk may help for we have within us a new appreciation of joy, of a new desire to create, of a *new will to be* . . . with *new determination* for all mankind."[63]

The great majority of American proletariat masses, however, rather than embrace this "new will" towards constituting an authentic human subjectivity-as-lived universal, were much more concerned with maintaining their 'white-as-universal subjectivity' of privilege in alliance with western imperialist power, than exercising any potential solidarity of ascendant humanity with Black people in popular emancipatory revolt.

Modernity, as organized, imposed and under-written by western imperialist power, and to which Marxism is itself epistemologically indebted, merely reinforces the subhumanity of Black people as *a priori* fact. "At the deepest level of Western knowledge, Marxism introduced no real discontinuity; it found its place without difficulty, as a full, quiet, comfortable and, goodness knows, satisfying form for a time (its own), within an epistemological arrangement that welcomed it gladly (since it was this arrangement that was in fact making room for it) and that it, in return, had no intention of disturbing and, above all, no power to modify, even

---

[63] DuBois, "Criteria of Negro Art", *The Crisis Magazine*, October 1926 (emphasis mine).

one jot, since it rested entirely upon it." [64] As such, the Harlem Renaissance, as a genuine aesthetic-ontological revolt asserting Black subjectivity-as-human 'being', introduced discontinuity within the normative gaze of a western imperialist continuum, and for which Marxism was also then very much ill prepared, namely because the socio-historical implications of such a "spiritual emancipation" as initiated by a people who already constitute a fundamental socio-ontological 'problem'[65] of modernity, radically outflanks "in tone" any previously rigid materialist eschatological narratives of geohistorical change which were slowly but surely becoming exposed as incapable of constituting the necessary human subjectivity to carry out a truly revolutionary "purpose".

Although definitely encouraging a retreat from the growing political militance of its day, the Harlem Renaissance is best understood as an even more radical phenomenon of socio-ontological re-orientation, an aesthetic rebellion and cultural reconstitution of human 'being' which effectively refused to barter away that relentless transcendence and spiritual upheaval which serve as the foundation of human endeavor (including revolutionary action), for yet another epistemological variant of

---

[64] Michel Foucault, *The Order of Things*, p.261.
[65] DuBois, *The Souls of Black Folk*, p.1-7.

that self-same 'white' subjectivity-as-universal which originates from a western imperialist continuum
and provides no new lived context which might
have dissuaded that savage 10,000 strong horde of
rational animality in Tulsa, Oklahoma who brutal-
ized an ascendant humanity through violent mob
terror aided by actual airplane raids resulting in
completely destroying the Black section of town
known as 'Little Africa' or 'Black Wallstreet' in
1921.[66]

Locke initiated *The New Negro* with an acute
discursive reconstitution of Black subjectivity-as-
human 'being' which then prepared the way for
DuBois, who had the last word in that very same
text, to globally situate this new Black subjectivity
within a more concrete socio-historical context, ultimately disclosing its exceptional antagonistic relation to a western imperialist continuum, and unveiling its topographical alterity in connection to
modernity itself. "Modern imperialism and modern
industrialism are one and the same system; root and
branch of the same tree. The race problem is the
other side of the labor problem; and the black man's
burden is the white man's burden. . . . remembering
always that *empire* is the heavy hand of capital
abroad. . . . This almost naïve setting of the *darker*

[66] Walter F. White, "The Eruption of Tulsa", *The Nation*, June 29,
1921; CXII, 909-10.

races beyond the pale of democracy and *of modern humanity* . . . involves two things – acquiescence of the darker peoples and agreement between capital and labor in white democracies."[67]   Empire, as the "heavy hand of capital", has since undergone a series of reconfigurations and to this day, has been able to sustain and prolong the "acquiescence of the darker peoples" who populate the socio-ontological underground of modernity, even while expansively globalizing the cooperative "agreement" with "labor", consequently assimilating state socialist and state communist opposition into a more complete and thorough hegemony of western imperialist power.

Thus, Locke and DuBois engaged in a dialectical gambit of the highest stakes, an epistemological gambit which temporarily suspended the historical justification of radical political agitation on aesthetic-cultural grounds, until such engagement necessarily encompassed not only the obvious economic exploitation of labor by capital, but also the racist dehumanization inherent in modernity itself, a dehumanization which socio-ontologically haunts even the redemptive claims of Marxist eschatology.[68]

---

[67] DuBois, "The Negro Mind Reaches Out", *The New Negro*, pp.386,402-403. Emphasis mine.
[68] Barbara Foley, *Spectres of 1919*: *Class & Nation in the Making of the New Negro*, (Urbana: University of Illinois Press, 2003, 2008). Justifiably critical of DuBois and Locke's dialectical

By initiating this aesthetic confrontation of modernity, a vast cultural reservoir of constitutive self-determination was unchained which would eventually prove vital in freeing radical Black subjectivity from becoming 'fixed' and ultimately trapped in yet another form of 'objecthood', which the prevailing and decidedly vulgar materialist perspective inherent throughout modernity before the advent of the Harlem Renaissance required. "In order to eliminate subjectivity, the materialist declares that he is an object, that is, the subject matter of science. But once he has eliminated subjectivity in favor of the object, instead of seeing himself as a thing among other things buffeted about by the physical universe, he makes himself an objective beholder and claims to contemplate nature as it is, in the absolute."[69]

Western imperialist power, whether expressed in advanced neo-liberal capitalism, military bureau-

---

gambit, Foley brilliantly examines the socio-historical tensions which informed the conditions that allowed Locke's vision of "the New Negro as cultural pluralist" to supercede the Marxist vision of "the New Negro as class-conscious warrior".

[69] Sartre, "Materialism and Revolution", *Literary and Philosophical Essays*, (New York: Collier Books, 1955, 1967) p.202. Sartre continues, "There is a play on the word objectivity, which sometimes means the passive quality of the object beheld and, at other times, the absolute value of a beholder stripped of subjective weaknesses. Thus, having transcended all subjectivity and identified himself with pure objective truth, the materialist travels about in a world of objects inhabited by human objects."

cratic communism, or naked fascism, cannot be effectively confronted or overcome through adherence to a set of deterministic presuppositions which are themselves derived solely from established structures of meaning and sanctioned epistemological foundations of a western imperialist continuum. The "racial mythology that accompanied capitalist industrial formation and provided its social structures engendered no truly profound alternatives. The social, ideological, and political oppositions generated within Western societies have proven unequal to the task"[70] and global scope of authentic human liberation.

By privileging a 'fixed' imperial anthropology of Man-as-rational animal, as mere 'objecthood' and 'empirical self' within a materialist eschatology of deterministic revolution, Revolt becomes exclusively enclosed within the normative gaze of modernity and suffocates any emancipatory potentialities that human 'being' might awaken, therefore ensuring that any genuine socio-historical movement towards human liberation has no ontological breath from which to sustain itself.

In the preface to the latest edition of *The New Negro*, Rampersad correctly states that Locke's text helped Harlem turn its back more firmly on radical

---

[70] Cedric Robinson, *Black Marxism: The Making of the Black Radical Tradition*, (Chapel Hill: University of North Carolina Press, 1983, 2000) p.316.

social movements. However, Rampersad's adherence to such conventional wisdom encourages a discursive blindness towards the socio-ontological necessity and dialectical nature of such an important epistemological reorientation. Already having experienced the brutal reifying attempts at reducing our human 'being' to mere 'objecthood' through *chattel* slavery, Black subjectivity-as-human 'being' sustains the socio-ontological imperatives of an ascendant humanity and necessarily rejects 'objecthood' in all its manifestations. 'Objecthood', even when cloaked in an emancipatory narrative of impending class-based revolution, is still nothing more than 'being-in-itself' overdetermined-from-without.

The assertion of Black subjectivity-as-human 'being' constitutes an exceptional antagonism in relation to modernity itself and therefore serves as a vast socio-ontological reservoir of insurgency for an ascendant humanity in continuous struggle and relentless confrontation with a western imperialist continuum. "This new humanity cannot do otherwise than define a new humanism both *for itself* and *for others*. It is prefigured both in the objectives and methods of conflict."[71]

Seizing upon this moment of constitutive self-determination, Lockean 'New Negro' cultural resistance against racist dehumanization spiritually emp-

---

[71] Fanon, *The Wretched of the Earth*, p.246. Emphasis mine.

owered and aesthetically functioned as a cultural pluralist fulcrum in discursive affirmation of an unbroken trajectory of Black Vindicationist historio-graphy[72] originating with the seminal contributions towards Black liberation discourse of David Walker and Frederick Douglass, which would subsequently assist in furthering a tremendous upsurge in histor-ical anthropology, social archaeology and cultural genealogy aimed at disclosing the all too human legacy of Black people which had been first necess-arily obscured, deformed and erased by a racist discourse and epistemology of established unjust global power, only to be reshaped and molded to fit the normative gaze of Empire.[73]

These efforts by Locke and DuBois however, no matter how socially effective in culturally preser-ving Black subjectivity-as-human 'being', ultimately ran the risk of necessarily limiting any immediate

[72] LaRose T. Parris, *Being Apart: Theoretical and Existential Resistance in Africana Literature*, (Charlottesville: University of Virginia Press, 2015) pp.4-8.
[73] Check out Carter G. Woodson, *The Mis-Education of the Negro*, (African American Images, 1933, 2000), J.A. Rogers, *World's Great Men of Color Vols.1&2*, (New York: Touchstone, 1946, 1996). George G.M. James, *Stolen Legacy*, (African American Images, 1954, 2001). Cheikh Anta Diop, *The African Origin of Civilization: Myth or Reality*, (Chicago: Lawrence Hill Books, 1967, 1974). John G. Jackson, *Introduction to African Civilizations*, (New York: Citadel Press, 1970, 1990). Martin Bernal, *Black Athena: The Afroasiatic Roots of Classical Civilization Vols.1&2*, (New Brunswick: Rutgers University Press, 1987, 1991).

emancipatory political aims by having made the "frequent mistake" of trying "to find cultural expressions for and to give new values to native culture within the framework of colonial domination."[74] Indeed, it would not be until that era of global grassroots emancipatory social upheavals associated with Black liberation praxis (often analytically framed through perspectives of 'civil rights', 'Black power' and decolonization movements) that the insurgent trajectory of "new values" and imperatives unleashed by Locke and DuBois would resonate with enough historical momentum and discursive clarity, to be re-enunciated and actualized in continuous resistance against the structural-inert "framework" of western imperialist power.

Black subjectivity-as-human 'being', as urgently upheld over centuries with the constitutive self-determining strength of Atlas braced against the massive sky of oppressive racist dehumanization, is informed by a socio-ontological depth of emancipatory commitment towards resisting the structural-inert violence and miseducation of soul which is inscribed into modernity as imposed by western imperialist power. This geohistorical resistance is the genesis of an insurgent epistemological reservoir which simultaneously validates potentialities for new paradigms of human 'being' and human

---

[74] Fanon, p.244.

liberation. "The struggle for freedom does not give back to the national culture its former values and shapes; this struggle which aims at a fundamentally different set of relations between men cannot leave intact either the form or the content of the people's culture. After the conflict there is not only the disappearance of colonialism but also the disappearance of the colonized man."[75]

As such, and definitively against the whims of Black hyperbourgeois sentimentality, the word 'nigger' does not need to be buried, for out of emancipatory necessity it will disappear on its own, following, if not during, though yet never preceding, the disappearance of the racist dehumanization and historical oppression from which it was discursively wrought to socio-ontologically cement upon human 'being'.

Indeed, what seems like a source of unlimited humor to some, as we have all heard such ignorant commentary that ridicules the constantly changing attempts at grasping lived Black experience (African – Slave – Nigger – Negro – Colored – Black – Afro-American – African-American – and Black again) within the rapid span of a few generations, is in actuality a very serious discursive effort by a socio-historically oppressed people whose ultimate aim is nothing short of authentic universal human lib-

[75] Fanon, p.246.

eration. Our assertion of Black subjectivity-as-human 'being' has been a constant and unyielding emancipatory narrative of continuing relevance to the contemporary geohistorical situation within modernity as imposed by western imperialist power. In resisting such overdetermination-from-without, we relentlessly find ourselves confronting and transcending a biopolitical alterity which pacifies 'who we are' while epistemologically chaining 'what we are' to those false materialist standards of human 'being': 'objecthood' and rational animality.

Recognizing our irreducible agency as situated consciousness and thus indistinguishable from the human condition, we deliberately carry the weight of a global responsibility for new potentialities of human 'being' as we determine what it means to constitute ourselves, facing our relentless transcendence, affirming our spiritual upheaval amidst the ebb, flow and disaster of history. We recognize ourselves as ascendant humanity by the very act of renouncing the pacification and overdetermination-from-without that weds our 'being-in-the-world' to a western imperialist continuum.

This latest effort to rid the world of the word 'nigger', is indicative of an effectively functioning dissimulative strategy of the normative gaze which allows for, and even encourages one to focus on and critique, unofficial 'popular' symbols of inferiority and injustice, so long as the actual structural-inert relations of power from which such signs gain sustenance and continued socio-historical legitimacy, remain unchallenged.

Any effort at constituting the socio-historical condition of genuine racist dehumanization as a sign, and then effortlessly behaving as though the sign itself, the word 'nigger', deserves existential primacy over the lived experience of oppression which gives it continued relevance by attempting to "abolish" it as a sign, is disingenuous. "The business of obscuring language is a mask which stands out the much greater business of plunder."[76] Even using the word "abolish", knowing full well the emancipatory connotations of such a word, and the discursive weight it carries in the Black diaspora, is at best irresponsible and at worst an effort at deliberate mystification of actual oppression. "Burying" the word 'nigger', by holding an actual funeral, a circus like event replete with 'civil rights' simulacra of indignant sentimentality, merely indicates the degree to which the NAACP is out of touch with the genuine emancipatory needs of our ascendant humanity as Black people. Are we struggling to be fully assimilated into a western imperialist continuum that we might receive our fair share of the spoils of oppression, and take our

---

[76] Fanon, p.189.

place as upstanding imperial citizens? Or are we on an emancipatory socio-ontological trajectory to bring about a truly just and egalitarian geonational community through an Overturning of Empire and a transcending of its racist anthropology towards human subjectivity-as-lived universal?

What does it tell us about the abdicating conscience of the Black hyperbourgeoisie, that it was a nonsensical racist stream of consciousness rant,[77] from a struggling 'white' slapstick comedian, pitifully unequipped with the wit, candor, intellectual capacity, and sense of humor to conduct a decent stand-up routine, that set this whole Spectacle in motion? Regardless of whether or not one agrees with the docile reformist tactics and assimilationist worldview of the hyperbourgeoisie, that the NAACP came up with this conformist reactionary carnival as a response to the racist ravings of a cornball 'white' comedian is either, in itself, sheer comedy, or epic tragedy.

There is so much more racist degeneracy to Michael Richards's rant than his vile use of the word 'nigger'. He began by telling the audience member, who had been heckling him, to "Shut Up!" Faced with a Black man who did not follow

---

[77] Transcription based on TMZ footage -
https://www.youtube.com/watch?v=BoLPLsQbdt0

established social norms and dared speak out of turn, he tried to shush him like one would an adolescent boy, by inducing him to silence with a verbal command from his authoritative position on stage.   Having failed in this initial discursive attempt to establish intersubjective control over a living example of that eternally unruly and prob-lematic Black subjectivity-as-human 'being', Rich-ards then wasted no time in reminding the young Black man of the very real potentialities of public ritual murder and biopolitical mob violence which have been historically used to discipline and punish the assertion of Black subjectivity-as-human 'being', or as he put it; "50 years ago we would have had you upside down with a fucking fork up your ass!".

Here Richards avoids directly confronting the Black man who heckled him by instead discursively pleading for ontic shelter in the "we" of his failed attempt to rally a bewildered herd of rational anim-ality under an ideological banner of 'whiteness'. Unfortunately, Richards also suffers from severe fits of 'wonderbread' cultural nationalist exceptional-ism that effectively veils his access to an authentic historical memory.   For in truth, be it James Byrd or Brandon McClelland,[78] to state only a couple of the most publicized incidents, you don't actually have

---

[78] "Black Man Dragged to Death in Texas", Larry Hales, *Workers World* (workers.org), October 30th, 2008.

to go back "50 years ago" to find instances where the lynching of human 'being' occurs.

What Michael Richards says next is extremely revealing. "You can talk, you can talk, you can talk! You're brave now motherfucker!" Choosing to engage in social discourse which challenges the normative gaze of modernity by asserting our human agency as Black people does indeed require a considerable degree of courage. For even the most trivial of situations, like heckling a 'wack@ss' comedian at a stand-up comedy club, might temporarily disrupt the topographical hierarchy of imperial coherence by way of 'racial incident' and thus attract the unaccountable violence of neocolonial police agents intent on recuperating and reconstituting the lived contours of western imperial power.

Richards's response is all the more severe because by the mere act of a Black man 'talkin sh*t', social disequilibrium is introduced within established structures of meaning by existentially committing a double foul in one discursive rupture: for by breaking away from conventions of courtesy between performer and audience during a public event, a Black man is inherently guilty of asserting that ever so 'problematic' Black subjectivity-as-human 'being' within the context of modernity which cloaks our 'being-in-the-world' with a coercive anonymity. Thus, the human agency of a Black man who is basically 'talkin sh*t and giving no f*cks' generates an existential panic from within Michael Richards, whose own identity of 'whiteness', as indicative of a potent biopolitical coalition between ruling power elite and working class masses, is discursively called into question hence rendering it profoundly, albeit only temporarily, inconsequential.

Richards's racist freestyle peaks in an attempt to dislocate and then dehumanize his Black antagonist in front of the rest of the audience with; "Throw his ass out, he's a nigger! He's a nigger! He's a nigger! A nigger, look there's a nigger!" In order to remove a Black man physically from his presence and restore the coloniality of topographical coherence between imperial mainstream-as-civil society and the socio-ontological underground, he attempts, through reliance on racist discourse meant to engender a biopolitical solidarity of 'whiteness' expressed in insulting language, to remove us from the human condition itself. By finding ontological guarantee in the normative gaze of western imperialist power as expressed in adherence to 'white' identity, Richards seeks to remind us of our place, our 'fixed' positionality of subhuman 'objecthood' derived from a vulgar materialist anthropological determinism of Man-as-rational animal.

Although the Black hyperbourgeoisie were ulti-mately embarrassed by Michael Richards' racist verbal attacks, for most postmodern lumpenprole-tariat brothers and sisters, our embarrassment origi-nates in the sheer inadequacy of that audience member's response to the situation. Why be sittin' there talkin' mad sh*t only to then 'catch feelings' when a cornball comedian loses his cool and inapp-ropriately calls you out, and then start complaining about how "that was uncalled for"? As if Richards' acknowledgement of having wronged him will alle-viate that existential burden on his soul which only resistance and emancipatory struggle can assuage. His response though disappointing, is not surpri-sing however, for we are all aware of that struc-tural-inert oppression which can erupt into violent praxis at any moment against the assertion of Black subjectivity-as-human 'being'. That brother, altho-ugh clearly adept at heckling the fool on stage, was no fool himself.

It's not that Michael Richards should have defi-nitively 'caught a bad one', no matter how justified. However, instead of continuing to 'talk sh*t' to Richards even more vociferously in response to being publicly berated, what we witnessed was an intersubjectively passive but socially safe response, reflecting a depressing lack of emancipatory agency which at times parasitically subsists in tandem with contemporary Black 'identity'. This is true especially when we find ourselves confronted with blatantly antagonistic examples of racism, which though publicly, loudly and symbolically are frowned upon as psychological aberrations of a bygone age, actually disclose an ever-lingering coherent topography of coloniality in the Raw as structural-inert relations of power between imperial mainstream and socio-ontological underground of modernity.

Michael Richards is not a member of the ruling power elite; he is the equivalent of a court jester forever existing at the compliant margins of the king's court, and this distance from power is the ultimate source of his rant and his racism. For the ruling power elite, racism is an ideological tool which camouflages historical relations of global power and maintains the coercive anonymity of structural-inert violence against those who by 'race' and coloniality find ourselves positioned as the socio-ontological underground of modernity. For the average 'empirical self' who is personally invested in 'white' subjectivity however, racism helps build a pragmatic alliance with established power and becomes a spiritual veil which masks a cancerous alienation from actual human 'being'. Richards's own intersubjective powerlessness before the discursive challenge to his stage presence at a comedy club by a rude heckler from the audience becomes transformed through his own comedic ineptness, into the brief ideological powerlessness of a once undisputed hegemony of 'whiteness' before the socio-ontological challenge to the normative gaze of established power by the assertion of Black subjectivity-as-human 'being'.

Unfortunately, the NAACP no longer has the capacity to marshal an emancipatory consensus around this exceptional antagonism, for it obviously takes pride in its own aptitude for absolute farce and socio-historical comedy, as it held a hyperreal funeral for the word 'nigger' complete with an actual burial.[79] I'm sure Black people everywhere rejoiced with feelings of tremendous exaltation knowing that somewhere in Detroit Memorial Park Cementary there is a headstone with the word 'nigger' on it. More hyperreal than the funeral itself however, were the words of some of the participants. Detroit Mayor Kwame Kilpatrick almost 'kept it real' when he suggested that we should be "burying all the things that go with the N-word." However, instead of following up with a thorough critique of advanced neo-liberal capitalist globalization and Empire, he fearlessly incited the crowd

---

[79] *Associated Press*, Monday July 9th, 2007.

with a vintage Blaxploitation homage to *The Mack*[80] by exhorting us to "bury the 'pimps' and the 'hos' that go with it." Not to be outdone in the hyper-reality of hyperbourgeois hyperbolic ranting, the good Rev. Otis Moss III, in a moment of pure ahistorical genius, claimed that the word 'nigger' "was the greatest child that racism ever birthed". Has bootlicking established power ever sounded so emancipatory?

Any movement of emancipatory praxis by Black people involves an authentic reconstitution of human 'being' that finds itself directly at odds with a structural-inert violence that grounds and binds the vested interests of a western imperialist continuum. Therefore, Black liberation praxis remains unimpressed, unmoved and unfulfilled by any cosmetic rearrangements of representative 'ethnic' populations allowed to assimilate further and further into a global cosmopolitan ruling power elite. The socio-ontological imperatives inherent in Black liberation demand an Overturning of modernity itself, towards a truly egalitarian geonational human community. As such, the only thing accomplished by this bogus funeral of the word 'nigger' was that more rhetorical 'civil rights' dust was kicked in the face of vast populations of Black people who are already

---

[80] A 'blaxploitation' motion picture directed by Michael Campus and written by Robert J. Poole, (Cinema Releasing Corp. 1973).

buried alive under an advanced neo-liberal capitalist tombstone of assimilation.

In truth, both words, 'nigger' and 'negro', are powerful semiotic referents within established structures of meaning signifying a discursive echo of that dehumanizing geohistorical brutality which is guilty of the murder of Man; a socio-ontological murder that is inscribed in modernity and continually reaffirms the normative gaze of a western imperialist continuum. And so, it matters not, that in "our virtual world, the question of the Real, of the referent, of the subject and its object, can no longer even be posed"[81] by Man-as-western bourgeois subjectivity. Indeed, the redemption of human 'being' now finds itself rooted in the socio-ontological underground of modernity that posits lived Black experience as a phenomenon that discloses universal potentialities of human subjectivity against the Real of globalized structural-inert violence.

[81] Baudrillard, *The Vital Illusion*, (New York: Columbia University Press, 2000) p.62.

don't make me smack the taste out your mouth – The cultural resilience of a myriad of linguistic inflections derived from the word 'nigger' within informal discourse amongst Black community throughout the Diaspora, suggests that the word 'nigger' is best understood, not as a definitive term belying a 'fixed' identity, but rather as a recurring and blatant reminder of the inherent racist dehumanization which is violently imposed upon us by western imperialist power. For regardless of whether heard in the berated slang of the postmodern lumpen-proletariat or in the familial humor which enriches the margins of any of our social encounters or cultural gatherings, the word 'nigger' invokes a certain spiritual vigilance over the manner in which we are solely responsible for the constitutive self-determination of our human 'being'.

Through its, often casual, invocation in the most random of our conversations, we are consistently reminded to be wary of the normative gaze of a western imperialist continuum which has never missed an opportunity to brazenly present the fruits of socio-historical oppression as the natural anthropological state of Black people. That oft heard refrain we hear, sometimes said to each other out of frustration, "to them you still a nigger", which is meant to supposedly hold us accountable to some essentialist racial authenticity, is in actuality a potent discursive referent amongst Black people, reminding us in no uncertain terms, that we will never be absolved of the human responsibility to continuously constitute ourselves in the face of a western imperialist continuum that was globally birthed through our racist dehumanization and is structurally maintained through our ontological disenfranchisement, mass incarceration and accumulative slaughter.

However, it should also be understood and clearly stated outright, without any hesitation or possible lament, that when such a potent discursive sign is misappropriated outside of its already displaced social or cultural context, and reinscribed with its original racist historical function of reifying the assertion of Black subjectivity-as-human 'being' into a 'fixed' dehumanizing 'objecthood', the chances of our all too human agency finding expression in a forceful reprisal comprised of an open handed rebuke across the countenance of such a well-meaning imbecile or ill-intentioned foe is indeed greatly increased.

global imperative for Black liberation praxis – As an unremitting socio-ontological Revolt against the bi-opolitical pacification imposed upon human 'being' by western imperialist power, the struggle for Black liberation provides an exacting geohistorical imper-ative towards insurgent potentialities of ascendant humanity against Empire.

Indeed, it is precisely because such emancipatory praxis is no longer as obviously globally prevalent, that the continued cultivation of Black liberation discourse is a worldwide dialectic necessity.

To be serious about Black liberation however, and the decisively relevant and universal human implications contained therein, does not require the resumption, no matter how crucial and important, of some preexisting 'race' struggle boisterously lob-bying for the imperial extension of liberal-dem-ocratic tolerance and demanding unequivocal cult-ural acceptance and economic assimilation into Empire as the ultimate aim of emancipatory praxis.

Nor does it necessitate the hasty appropriation of archaeo-nostalgic value systems mined from an essentialist locus of classical Afroasiatic tradition and culture. For though socially urgent and cultur-ally indispensable, the epistemological demands of scholarly research into historical truth buried deep under the legitimizing shrouds of the normative gaze, should not be regarded as possessing enough of an insurrectionary force from which to cull the emancipatory imperatives needed to embark on a trajectory of confrontation against western imperialist power.

Rather, such a confrontation with a western imperialist continuum entails a geonational project of emancipatory praxis willed for by the relentless transcendence of human 'being', in all its universality, fully cognizant of the coloniality in the Raw which exists as the socio-ontological guarantee of established unjust globalized power, and the structural-inert violence and miseducation of soul which maintain the normative gaze and preserve the Real of human suffering as an ahistorical constant of Empire.

enunciations of Revolt – Universal consent is no requisite for geohistorical insurrection. Overemphasis on discovering a 'fixed' totality of objective social conditions from which to rationally impose scientific rigor and mathematical precision upon historical events, as politically inevitable 'revolution' generated by mechanistic economic contradictions hemmed up within the boundaries of a particular nation-state, inherently hinders socio-ontological potentialities for constituting human subjectivity commensurate with the genesis of *insurrection-for-itself.*

Laundered throughout academia as an oppositional stance without an insurgent trajectory, 'revolution' risks becoming a commodified plaything, a fetishistic pastime, an eschatological construct for a sedentary and parasitic amalgamation of pigeon-holed bureaucrats, scholarly experts and crumb snatching *uber*specialists, hiding behind precepts of intellectual quietism, while exhibiting socio-ontological cowardice whenever delegitimizing geohistorical Revolt that refuses to conform towards dogmatic theoretical presumptions as epistemologically sanctioned by a western imperialist continuum. These *chiens de garde*[82] are much more likely to riot for a tenured position within a sanctioned academic

---

[82] Paul Nizan, *The Watchdogs*, (New York: Monthly Review Press, 1961).

institution of a socio-political system they claim to struggle so virulently against, than get their pens dirty and implicate their notebooks and laptops by engaging themselves as intellectuals towards actual emancipatory praxis against Empire.[83]

Indeed, emancipatory praxis undermines the topographical coherence of structural-inert violence and miseducation of soul which sustains the normative gaze, and hence upsets the very pretext from which they derive their credentialed authority.

However, it is only insofar as the Academy is not an ivory tower leaning towards disinterested pursuit of knowledge that it should be reproached. For such a fate is indicative of more radical possibilities than pragmatic fulfillment of the restorative epistemological needs of the imperial mainstream-as-civil society. Indeed, does not even the very fetishization of genuine radical discourse within the Academy simultaneously preserve the long-range epistemological potency of that which it momentarily curtails from lived historical immediacy?

Authentic enunciations of Revolt open out towards socio-historical relevance, informing lived trajectories of human subjectivity and revealing new horizons of emancipatory praxis, thereby heightening potentialities of insurrection-for-itself. "There's

---

[83] David L. Schalk, *War and the Ivory Tower*, (Lincoln: University of Nebraska Press, 1991, 2005).

something more dangerous about attacking the pigs of the power structure verbally than there is in walking into the Bank of America with a gun and attacking it forthrightly."[84] Here, Cleaver's allusion towards "something more dangerous" discloses an epistemological crisis which erupts during attempts at enunciating the socio-ontological imperative towards Revolt ignited by the assertion of Black subjectivity-as-human 'being'. For the geohistorical imperative of Black liberation overwhelms in scope the normative gaze of a western imperialist continuum which informs and regulates that which can be discursively conceptualized. As such, uninformed action is just as much a debasement of emancipatory praxis as irrelevant theory, even when uninformed action finds itself in direct confrontation with a representative institution of advanced neo-liberal capitalism ie. "walking into the Bank of America with a gun".

---

[84] Eldridge Cleaver, *Post-Prison Writings & Speeches*, (New York: Vintage, 1969) p.150.

Oscar Grant, Lovelle Mixon and implicated temporality
– A certain and brutal death awaits Oscar Grant
while neo-colonial police force his face down to the
floor and pull his arms behind his back, thus violently subduing him into compliance to the sovereign legitimacy of Empire. This in spite of Grant's
measured and tactical response of acquiescence to
the orders of neo-colonial police agents, who regularly exercise objective violence against any assertion of Black subjectivity-as-human 'being' while
patrolling the constantly shifting positional coherence of imperial topography. Tragically, such measured acquiescence ultimately fails in preventing his
execution style death by a point-blank gunshot to
his back.

What recourse then remains, for those of us
whose 'being-in-the-world' indulges a tentative cultural commerce of acquiescence to western imperialist power, towards the mere suggested possibility
of bare survival and cheap spiritual leisure? Has
turning our gaze away from the horizon of emancipatory praxis really brought an end to the globalized oppression of human 'being' we Black people
suffer in coercive anonymity? The murder of Oscar
Grant discloses the Raw of coloniality as a pitiless
biopolitical alterity existing between imperial mainstream of modernity and the socio-ontological underground that is consistently veiled by the normative gaze of Empire.

Since acquiescence fails to keep us alive, do efforts to more vigorously resist neo-colonial police violence preserve our life? Does resistance change the murderous outcome of our encounters with neo-colonial 'law enforcement'? Is there any geohistorical value or socio-ontological insight into the human condition which is revealed by our resistance? Does resistance open potentialities of sustaining human subjectivity against the tyranny of objective violence inscribed in modernity, even at the risk of succumbing to the inherent mortality of human 'being'? Assertion of human agency may indeed lead to an untimely death, even as the spiritual integrity of emancipatory praxis may be all that distinguishes and sustains our trajectory of human subjectivity against a more complete socio-ontological decimation of existence.

Lovelle Mixon chose to resist the tyranny of structural-inert violence by constituting his human subjectivity against western imperialist power through lumpenproletariat vendetta as force of arms against neo-colonial police, ultimately ensuring four police officers never return from the precipice of anomie along with him. And yet, in what sense is the singular legitimacy of Mixon's all too human response to oppression made possible by the very ethical ambiguity and legal indeterminacy which mediates against any clear distinction existing between justified spiritual resentment spontaneously erupting as lumpenproletariat vendetta, and socio-ontological imperatives for insurgent historical transformation unleashed through emancipatory praxis against Empire?

The normative gaze of established power constitutes the murder of Man as necessarily objective violence permeating modernity in its contemporary guise of advanced neo-liberal capitalist globalization. This structural-inert violence is unsustainable without racist dehumanization as the very condition of its possibility. Indeed, genuine recognition of our shared humanity pierces through veils of coercive anonymity which makes no distinction between Oscar Grant and Lovelle Mixon: both were murdered for that 'problematic' assertion of Black subjectivity-as-human 'being'. As such, there are no absolute ethical considerations informing diverse modes of resistance, by which to safely guide emancipatory praxis away from the reach of a vast and violent apparatus of oppression. The assertion of Black subjectivity-as-human 'being' explicitly discloses the truth of our shared human condition as implicated temporality which acquaints our existence with untimely death and perpetual incarceration. Not as accidental occurrences, but as geo-historical consequences of an ascendant humanity situated within the confines of a pervasive western imperialist continuum.

The Black Panther Party for Self-Defense and Black Liberation Army[85] are now a distant bitter memory, having been socially persecuted through political imprisonment and torture, functionally annihilated by counterinsurgent campaigns of para-militarized policing and ideologically discredited by the normative gaze of Empire. Since their resounding neutralization, which deliberately coin-cides with the sovereign appropriation of formerly non-aligned nations within Empire, we now expe-rience that ominous unaccountability and objective violence of neo-colonial police force in the solitude of knowing that there exists no geohistorically legitimate organized form of armed resistance to the imperatives of established power accessible to *the wretched of the earth* who constitute the socio-onto-

---

[85] Bobby Seale, *Seize the Time*, (Baltimore: *Black Classic Press*, 1968, 1996). Reginald Major, *A Panther is a Black Cat: An Account of the Early Years of the Black Panther Party – Its Origins, Its Goals, and Its Struggle for Survival*, (Baltimore: *Black Classic Press*, 1971, 2007). *The Black Panther Party [Reconsidered]*, edited by Charles E. Jones, (Baltimore: *Black Classic Press*, 1998, 2005). *Liberation, Imagination, and the Black Panther Party*, edited by Kathleen Cleaver and George Katsiaficas, (New York: *Routledge*, 2001). Joshua Bloom and Waldo E. Martin, Jr., *Black Against Empire,* (Berkeley: University of California Press, 2013), Sekou Odinga, Dhoruba Bin Wahad, Shaba Om, Jamal Joseph, *Look For Me in the Whirlwind: From the Panther 21 to 21st-Century Revolutions*, (Oakland: PM Press, 2017).

logical underground of modernity. This vacuum is the very condition of possibility for the growing frequency of postmodern lumpenproletariat vendettas against neo-colonial police.

Whether in acquiescence or resistance to the dictates of neo-colonial police, the ever-present possibility of untimely death remains an infallible concern. As such, to acquiesce is to gamble on the benevolence of the oppressor, to resist is to wager upon the inviolable truth of the human condition. Pursuit of emancipatory praxis is no safe haven from injustice, and yet neither is lying face down with our hands wrapped behind our back. The inevitability of this impossible decision confronts us with the dread of actualizing our human 'being' as irreducible agency and assuming responsibility for the insurgent trajectory of our human subjectivity against the gratuitous prospects of violent biopolitical persecution by Empire.

Insurrection-in-itself serves as an emancipatory counterweight to the murder of Oscar Grant, by Returning the objective violence of oppression back upon itself through protest-as-resistance and spontaneous rebellion in utter rejection of a geohistorical quietism that seeks to veil the murder of Man.

While we obviously have unprecedented access to much more avenues of media technology with which to document and unveil the sanctioned accumulated slaughter of ascendant humanity, what remains quietly elusive and seemingly inaccessible to us, out of sheer dread and trepidation over the prestige of Empire, is that choice to channel the irreducibility of human agency and inspire the radical imagination towards any relevant socio-historical potentialities of emancipatory praxis beyond all too evident choices of protest-as-resistance and spontaneous rebellion as insurrection-in-itself.

protest-as-resistance versus protest-as-ritual event –
Empire siphons away creative intensity and insurgent potentialities of protest-as-resistance by prag-
matically sanctioning a rational plurality of emotionally cathartic opportunities for 'liberal-democratic'
passion plays enacting protest-as-ritual event within the imperial mainstream-as-civil society. This
serves to consolidate the sovereign legitimacy and
further cement the hegemony of a western imperialist continuum.[86]

Protest-as-resistance involves an unrepentant
arrogation of sovereign legitimacy by an ascendant
humanity that confronts the normative gaze of
established power with an emancipatory gaze of
Revolt. By deliberately disrupting the accumulated
simulacra of ahistorical quietism, protest-as-resistance effectively challenges, pushes back and imposes an insurgent pressure to bear upon the topographical coherence of Empire, at times liberating
socio-ontological horizons of struggle towards allowing the relentless transcendence and spiritual
upheaval of human 'being' to constitute new poten-

[86] "These demonstrations are not confrontations when they remain
within the framework of legality. But when they do so, they
subject themselves to the institutionalized violence that
autonomously determines the framework of legality and can
restrict it to a suffocating minimum . . . And then the opposition
is placed before the fatal decision: opposition as ritual event or
opposition as resistance i.e. civil disobedience." Herbert Marcuse,
Five Lectures, (Boston: Beacon Press, 1970) p.89.

tialities of human subjectivity-as-lived universal through emancipatory praxis.

Our contemporary era is spiritually stigmatized
by a mass abdication of human agency that coalesces with an unencumbered technological fetish.
And yet, are we not now bearing witness to new
emancipatory dispositions of human subjectivity,
being decisively reborn through an undifferentiated
choice of rebellion against globalized structural-
inert violence mediated by greater access to technology?   Are not the same brothers and sisters
engaged in diligently fitting, sealing and wrapping
waste cotton over glass bottles containing three
fourths kerosene and one fourths motor oil, also
communicating and organizing via the same smart-
phone message encryption used by the global cosmopolitan capitalist elite?[87]

Have we lost such faith in the radical imagination,
that we no longer recognize our own all too human
face, when half covered by bandanas or folded T-
shirts, leaving neo-colonial police agents with lasting impressions of intersubjective resonance from
our unrepentant emancipatory gaze? Why should
we dismiss the courage and inspiration disclosed by
our brothers and sisters who sparingly splash gaso-
line on those fitted glass bottles, right before ignit-

---

[87] Josh Halliday, "London Riots: How BlackBerry Messenger
played a key role", *The Guardian* (theguardian.com), August 8,
2011.

ing and choosing to constitute fresh potentialities of human subjectivity by throwing Molotov cocktails against such an overwhelming counterinsurgent deployment of neo-colonial police force?[88]   These massive armed shows of force explicitly reveal counterinsurgent reconfigurations of western imperialist power, thereby potently reminding us, not only of that which persists, but also of that which is at stake, when the assertion of Black subjectivity-as-human 'being' breaches the blockade of symbolic cultural forms and engages the naked primacy of history.

A Molotov cocktail thrown against globalized structural-inert injustice breaks into flaming shards. Our emancipatory inhibitions shatter along with it, as socio-historical movement towards insurrection-in-itself, like burning kerosene, intersubjectively resonates throughout a western imperialist continuum, spreading by tides of fire.   As a rebirth of human subjectivity-as-lived universal draws nearer, can geonational insurrection-for-itself be too far behind?

---

[88] Paul D. Shinkman, "Ferguson and the Militarization of Police", *U.S. News & World Report* (usnews.com), August 14, 2014.

naked mask of the Divine – Faced with a brutal structural-inert globalized oppression as historically ushered into fruition through the violent imposition of modernity by western imperialist power, and the continuing epistemological authority corresponding to an anthropology of racist dehumanization, the cultivation of human subjectivity-as-lived universal, which might arise and shoulder the weight of insurrection-for-itself towards geonational egalitarian human community, finds socio-ontological refuge in the Divine as emancipatory imperatives existing beyond the scope of Empire.

However, by Divine imperatives, is not meant a conjuring up of excessive immateriality or idealism in the absolute, thus cloaking existence within an essentialist irresponsibility nurtured by religious dogma. For the Divine appears to consciousness masked in an exclusive breaching of existence by way of human 'being' that manifests a socio-historical nakedness of dialectic movement as call and response in mediation against the Real through emancipatory praxis as the very condition of its possibility.

atheism, Empire and the Divine – Atheism sweeps up the battered stained glass shards of blind fanaticism and dilapidated institutional refuse of absolute dogma, as generated from past religious dispensations in direct correlation to a thorough political assimilation of outward religious forms by established power towards spiritually legitimating the social scope of its claims to historical sovereignty. For as religious authority inevitably cedes primacy of the Divine towards becoming an effective translation of the normative gaze of Empire, that originary lived spiritual vitality associated with the socio-historical phenomenon of Divine Revelation becomes unsustainable, and in dire need of renewal through emancipatory praxis. As such, atheism revels in inauthenticity when divorced from a radical critique of the normative gaze of established power as an unsurpassable and absolute horizon of meaning.

Indeed, an atheism without emancipatory orientation, dangerously courts reductionist anthropological postures of epistemic closure[89] in absolute denunciation of the Divine, hence justifying 'objecthood', and thereby silencing insurgent rhythms of human 'being' towards emancipatory praxis against Empire.

---

[89] "Epistemic closure is a moment of presumably complete knowledge of a phenomenon. Such presumed knowledge closes off efforts at further inquiry." Lewis R. Gordon, *What Fanon Said*, (New York: Fordham University Press, 2015) p.49.

Atheism, as a metaphysical choice of retreat from the Divine, finds historical bearing within a lived trajectory of social subservience and epistemological deference to established power. Indeed, atheism increases the vulnerability of human 'being' to the normative gaze of Empire by reifying a materialist determinism that enables an ontological abdication of human subjectivity and thereby "violates the most general principle of all religions, the sanctity and inviolability of the subjective frame of mind."[90]

The Douglassian anti-slavery dialectic affirms the emancipatory prominence of human subjectivity as a "heaven of comparative freedom" and "spirit . . . roused to an attitude of independence";[91] and it is this inviolable human subjectivity which serves as an indispensable socio-ontological reservoir of Revolt. As such, "the religion of the slaves was a public matter ... State legislatures passed laws concerning the practice of slave religion. Masters controlled the slaves' religion by providing white ministers or observing the preaching of Black ministers. There was a general fear that allowing slaves the opportunity to experience religion in their own way would lead to revolts, the abolition of slavery, or perhaps, at least as they saw it, the destruction of civilization

---

[90] Karl Marx, "Remarks On the New Instructions to the Prussian Censors", (1842). www.marxists.org

[91] Douglass, *Autobiographies*, p.591.

itself."[92]   Indeed, that kinetic distance of interiority, that 'presence-towards-self' as situated consciousness, discloses the human condition as irreducible agency towards the cultivation of emancipatory praxis against a western imperialist continuum; far more insurgent in scope than blind faith in a materialistic determinism of economic contradictions and eschatological belief in a messianic working class.

Thus, an atheism bereft of emancipatory orientation functions as epistemological hygiene within the imperial mainstream, undermining "the *expression* of real suffering and a *protest* against real suffering", muting "the sigh of the oppressed creature," reifying "the heart of a heartless world," and hence pacifying "the soul of soulless conditions"[93] from voicing an insurgent Yearning of consciousness resonating from the underground of modernity as an existential catalyst towards imperatives of Divine justice.   That is, imperatives towards constituting a diverse geonational egalitarian human community beckoning emancipatory praxis towards socio-historical movement beyond structures of meaning imposed by a western imperialist continuum.

---

[92] *Encyclopedia of Slave Resistance and Rebellion Vol.2*, edited by Junius P. Rodriguez, (Westport: Greenwood Press, 2007) p.425.

[93] Marx, "Contribution to the Critique of Hegel's Philosophy of Right", (1844). www.marxists.org

As such, the Divine, even when corresponding to the Cause of God,[94] cannot be fully grasped as a scientific hypothesis subject to rational scrutiny, even when welcoming interrogations of reason against the dictates of blind fanaticism towards challenging the institutional sedimentation of dogmatic absolutism. Rather, the Divine summons human agency towards a wager of the highest stakes based upon recognition that the Real, as that which is empirically measurable and evidently manifest, does not exhaust the lived horizon of socio-historical potentialities as singularly disclosed through the constitutive self-determination, relentless transcendence and spiritual upheaval of human 'being' engaged in emancipatory praxis against Empire.

----

[94] My own theological reading of Bahai Faith posits 'the Cause of God' as an unceasing dialectic of Divine Revelation and humanity, 'the Religion of God' as evolving geohistorically situated stages of communal praxis in engagement with Divine Revelation, and 'the Faith of God' as an existentially mediated singular praxis of human 'being' faced with potentialities of recognizing Divine Revelation. Other theological engagements with Bahai Faith can be found in Nader Saiedi, *Logos and Civilization*, (Bethesda: University Press of Maryland, 2000) and Udo Schaefer, *The Light that Shineth in Darkness*, (Oxford: George Ronald, 1977).

beheading Freudian anthropology – Freudian anthropology,[95] as the conception of Man which informs
psychoanalytic theory, translates socio-historically
situated characteristics of a western bourgeois psyche divided into "new biological hypotheses"[96] that
posit an immutable psychological permanence of
universal human nature which *a priori* renders Black
subjectivity as incompatible with authentic human
'being'. Hence, psychological paradigms based on
this presupposition of an unsurpassable gulf between 'conscious/ego' and 'unconscious/id' censored
by a 'superego', cement Man-as-western bourgeois
subjectivity and preserve a coherent topography of
oppressive hierarchal relations of coloniality between imperial mainstream and socio-ontological underground of modernity.

Gordon's thought here is crucial, "If psychoanalysis cannot articulate Black reality in psycho-

---

[95] "I am not referring to the particular science called
anthropology, which is the study of cultures exterior to our own;
by 'anthropology' I mean the strictly philosophical structure
responsible for the fact that the problems of philosophy are now
all lodged within the domain that can be called human finitude. If
one can no longer philosophize about anything but man insofar as
he is a *Homo natura*, or in so far as he is a finite being, to that
extent isn't every philosophy at bottom an anthropology? This
being the case, philosophy becomes the cultural form within
which all the sciences of man in general are possible." Michel
Foucault, *Aesthetics, Method, and Epistemology*, (New York: The
New Press, 1994, 1998) p.250.
[96] Sigmund Freud, *An Outline of Psychoanalysis*, (New York:
W.W. Norton & Company, 1949, 1969) p.81.

analytic terms without being fallacious, then the baggage of societal foundations associated with psychoanalysis – namely, sexuality, gender, filial life – are also problematic bases of a body politic that militates against the presence of the Black."[97] Freudian anthropology is thus implicated as fundamentally without justification when faced with the assertion of Black subjectivity-as-human 'being'.

As such, the all too human phenomenon of lived Black experience lays bare the neck of psychoanalytic anthropology for a guillotine of existential liberation critique to cut through the Freudian conception of Man towards that objectifying onus of biological determinism, a vulgar materialist onus of biological determinism which exerts such a profound dehumanizing weight upon not only psychoanalysis, but the entire epistemological trajectory of modernity. For as Fanon discloses, "what is important to us here is to show that with the Negro the cycle of the biological begins."[98] Behold the threshold of the biopolitical.

The threshold of this biopolitical "cycle" is historically rooted in the cauldron of *chattel* slavery

---

[97] Lewis R. Gordon, "The Black and the Body Politic: Fanon's Existential Phenomenological Critique of Psychoanalysis", included in *Fanon: A Critical Reader*, edited by Lewis R. Gordon, T. Denean Sharpley-Whiting (Oxford: Blackwell Publishing, 1996) p.80.
[98] Fanon, *Black Skin, White Masks*, p.161.

that systematically endeavored towards the reduction of human 'being' to mere matter. It cannot plausibly be ignored that this explicit materialist reification of human 'being', this pointed and thorough translation of situated consciousness into 'objecthood', for the express purpose of exchanging humanity as commodity, was not only an economic vehicle which generated vast reserves of capital across global networks,[99] but an important epistemological foundation of modernity and socio-ontological praxis of coloniality, all functioning together as the very condition of possibility for a western imperialist continuum.

This "cycle of the biological", as ushered in by the fulcrum of modernity, eroded vast potentialities of human 'being' through an "avalanche of murders" that culminated in the biopolitical constitution of "Man in the technique and style of Europe".[100] As Foucault clarifies, "the threshold of our modernity is situated not by the attempt to apply objective methods to the study of man, but rather by the constitution of an empirico-transcendental doublet which was called *man*."[101] However, the discursive constitution of this "doublet" conceptually obscures an existential closure of human

[99] Eric Williams, *Capitalism and Slavery*, (Chapel Hill: University of North Carolina Press, 1944, 1994).
[100] Fanon, *The Wretched of the Earth*, p.312.
[101] Foucault, *The Order of Things*, p.319.

'being' that occurs as potentialities of freedom become subordinate to deterministic instincts of rational animality. Human agency thus yields to the causal mechanisms of an 'empirical self'; at lived expense of our 'presence-towards-self', that vital rhythm of constitutive self-determination, relentless transcendence and spiritual upheaval by which human 'being' moves towards a continuous becoming of human subjectivity.

It is no mere accident that 'race', as that rational signification of subhumanity, is explicitly embroiled in this constitution of an "empirico-transcendental doublet" which serves as a potent epistemological referent for a western imperialist continuum as natural and ahistorical. For it is only after the initiation of a western imperialist continuum as global praxis, that the normative gaze of established power finds it necessary to posit "the value of the empirical at the transcendental level",[102] thus ossifying the culmination of human neurobiological evolution into Man-as-western bourgeois subjectivity, and permanently 'fixing' the violently over-determined subhumanity of non-western subjectivity as an empirically evident 'fact' of modernity.

Freudian psychoanalytic theory, as an exemplary working model of positing "the empirical at the transcendental level", fundamentally alters and

---

[102] Foucault, p.320.

precisely shapes a type of discourse allowing for a gradual displacement of human agency through the power of a deterministic 'unconscious' that "expresses the true purpose of the individual organism's life".[103] This concerted war of psychological attrition on human agency continues today in a vast and ever expanding marketplace of therapeutic culture that Freud helped spawn, and which still provides psychoanalysis with its popular ideological influence over an ever growing and ever more global public.

At an epistemological level, however, the Freudian hypothesis of a deterministic 'unconscious', as an unquestioned dogmatic 'fact' of modernity, allows psychoanalysis to continue exerting an impressive theoretical influence on the normative gaze that perpetually constitutes and consolidates the hegemony of western imperialist power, as exemplified in the Academy by the effects of the Freudian turn upon the entire field of the human sciences.[104]

---

[103] Freud, *An Outline of Psychoanalysis*, p.17.

[104] "This problem of the unconscious is really very difficult, because apparently one can say that psychoanalysis is a form of psychology that is added to the psychology of consciousness, doubling the psychology of consciousness with a supplementary layer that would be that of the unconscious. And, as a matter of fact, it was realized immediately that by discovering the unconscious one pulled in at the same time a lot of problems that no longer involved either the individual, exactly, or the soul opposed to the body; but that one brought back inside the strictly psychological problematic what had previously been excluded

Psychoanalysis thus provides established power with an important ideological locus from which to reify displacement of the socio-historical origins of mental pathology suffered by *the wretched of the earth* populating the socio-ontological underground of modernity. Veiled in the rigid categorical neutrality of objective scientific discourse, Freudian psychoanalysis allows for an inverted translation of psychological trauma and socio-ontological wounds originating from globalized structural-inert oppression against human 'being', into biological impulses and primordial drives originating from an 'empirical self-as-rational animal', therefore neutralizing any potentialities of rupture from the normative gaze of Empire. This blatant psychological inversion, by positing empirical values at the level of transcendence, assists with the coercion of Black subjectivity-as-human 'being' into anonymity, by displacing the structural-inert violence inscribed in

---

from it, either on the grounds that it was physiology, reintroducing the problem of the body, or sociology, reintroducing the problem of the individual with his milieu, the group to which he belongs, the society in which he is caught, the culture in which he and his ancestors have always thought. With the result that the simple discovery of the unconscious is not an addition of domains: it is not an extension of psychology, it is actually the appropriation, by psychology, of most of the domains that the human sciences covered – so that one can say that starting with Freud, all the human sciences became, in one way or another, sciences of the psyche." Foucault, *Aesthetics, Method and Epistemology*, p.252.

modernity from its geohistorical roots, rendering it visible as banality, in safe objective harmony with the Real, and as such, a rather obvious, superfluous 'fact' to be acknowledged, only the better to be dismissed.

However, "the root of mental pathology must be sought not in some kind of metapathology, but in a certain relation, historically situated, of man to the mad man and to the true man."[105] Unraveling this Foucauldian knot requires a socio-historically situated understanding of "man" as the dominated non-resisting bewildered masses; in relation to "the mad man" suffering from the sheer insanity of daring to assert Black subjectivity-as-human 'being' against the normative gaze of a western imperialist continuum which is incarnated in the "the true man" as western bourgeois subjectivity.

An almost literal exemplification of this occurred during a previous era of massive social unrest, when cases of "protest psychosis" innocently and spontaneously appeared as "a term used in psychiatric literature in the 1960's by white doctors in New York. It basically categorized Black men who were participating in civil rights as insane. It was a way

---

[105] Foucault, *Mental Illness and Psychology,*(Berkeley: Univ. of California Press, 1954, 1987) p.2.

to pathologize the civil rights protest."[106] If the 'civil rights by moral suasion' front of the Black liberation movement were regarded as clinically insane, the 'human rights by any means necessary' front must have appeared as incontrovertible proof of genuine extraterrestrial 'being' originating from another planet entirely.

Freudian psychoanalytic theory contributes to the normative gaze of established power by regulating socially legitimate and recognizable psychological attributes for a 'fixed' anthropology whose ultimate aim is to maintain a perfect equilibrium within a western imperialist continuum. Few are thus surprised that "doctors diagnosed schizophrenia in African-American patients, and particularly African-American men, four times as often as in white patients", and since the psychological condition of 'schizophrenia' is framed in medical discourse as "the most biologically based of the mental illnesses" with symptoms such as "delusions, hallucinations, disorganized speech, disorganized or catatonic behavior, or so-called negative symptoms such as affective flattening – to defects in specific brain structures, peptides or neurotransmitters"; how can the sanity of Black people not come under

---

[106] From "Schizophrenia as Political Weapon", an interview by Felicia Pride of Jonathan M. Metzl for *The Root Magazine* (theroot.com), January 25, 2010.

'medically objective' psychological scrutiny?[107]   Indeed, how can we forget that the assertion of Black subjectivity-as-human 'being' is itself rendered pathological in relation to modernity as a 'problem' and 'biopolitical danger'?

Epistemological capitulation to the Freudian postulate of an 'id' and its complimentary psychological categories of an 'ego' and 'superego', in an ongoing melee with a 'life instinct' and a 'death drive', contributes towards a normative anthropological model of an 'empirical self-as-rational animality' which reasserts the historical hegemony of western bourgeois subjectivity as a universal standard of human 'being'; beginning with the 'savage' primal hordes of a mythic past and culminating into an even more mythic present of a 'civilized' West.[108] Such epistemological capitulation allows the structural-inert violence of western imperialist power to appear simultaneously as both historical banality and evolutionary triumph.[109]

---

[107]Jonathan M. Metzl, *The Protest Psychosis: How Schizofrenia Became a Black Disease*, (Boston: Beacon Press, 2011) p.x.

[108] Sigmund Freud, *Civilization and its Discontents*, (New York: Doubleday Anchor Books, 1930, 1958).

[109] "Psychoanalysis, in pertaining to non-Western countries, is always imbricated with anthropology(as ethnopsychology), which largely precludes the specificity (and thus normativity) of the object of study." Then after backtracking a little bit, things get very interesting from an existential liberationist perspective: ". . . this exclusion need not mean that we should jettison psychoanalysis since it is perhaps our most elaborate language of

The hypothesis of a deterministic 'unconscious' continues to be extremely influential and is THE fundamental characteristic of Freudian anthropology. This hypothesis constitutes an essentially unquestioned dogmatic ideological presupposition of modernity and functions as an ahistorical burial ground of existential freedom and social responsibility for each 'empirical self-as-rational animality'. This psychological presumption of an 'unconscious', cushions the fall from grace inherent whenever Man-as-western bourgeois subjectivity takes account of his own bloodstained hands that savagely fasten a 'white' mask upon the face of humanity. A pale mask of 'race' that alienates lived experience and objectifies the human condition in biopolitical adherence to false standards of human 'being'.

The collective memory of western imperialist savagery and barbarism against humanity finds in Freudian psychoanalysis an effective epistemological hygiene that cleanses the imperial mainstream from any psychological disposition betraying an intersubjective resonance of empathy towards *the wretched of the earth*, thus impeding solidarity with the increasing socio-ontological weight of historical disequilibrium introduced into modernity by the

subject constitution." Kalpani Seshadri-Crooks, "The Primitive as Analyst: Postcolonial Feminism's Access to Psychoanalysis", *Cultural Critique* #28, p.175-218.

assertion of Black subjectivity-as-human 'being'. Indeed, "psychoanalysis substitutes for the notion of bad faith, the idea of a lie without a liar"[110], which ultimately correlates to an imperial mainstream of modernity which is structurally saturated with racism, yet without a racist in sight.[111]

Furthermore, the methodological postulation of an 'unconscious', which can only be accessed with professional assistance by a psychoanalyst, at once establishes a potent formula for social control in which the very "core of our being . . . has no direct communication with the external world and is accessible even to our own knowledge only through the medium of another agency"[112] which just happens to be complicit with and legitimated by Empire.

Suddenly however, an odd experience of déjà vu arises upon the realization that Freudian psychoanalysis dogmatically suggests that an authentic knowledge of the human condition is only attainable through ceding spiritual autonomy to the normative gaze of a western imperialist continuum "which yields him no true self-consciousness, but only lets him see himself through the revelation of the other world. It is a peculiar sensation this

---

[110] Sartre, *Being and Nothingness*, p.49.
[111] For more on the relation between Sartrean Bad Faith and racist dehumanization, check out Lewis R. Gordon, *Bad Faith and Antiblack Racism*, (Amherst: Humanity Books, 1999).
[112] Freud, *An Outline of Psychoanalysis*, p.84.

double consciousness, this sense of always looking at one's self through the eyes of others, of measuring one's soul by the tape of a world that looks on in amused contempt and pity."[113]   Under the influence of Freudian anthropology, the singularity of 'being-in-the world' is rendered psychologically unauthorized to perceive the Real, and henceforth epistemologically reliant on "another agency" sanctioned by structural-inert global power. Is this not a therapeutic cloning of Duboisian 'double consciousness' that torments lived Black experience within modernity, socio-ontologically watered down, and discursively packaged as a psychological breakthrough?

Indeed, although discursively veiled as both scientific method and therapeutic imperative towards understanding the hidden inaccessible "core of our being", Freudian psychoanalytic theory assumes, revalorizes and further contributes towards the psychological reification of our 'presence-towards-self' into an 'empirical self-as-rational animality' that is endemic to modernity as imposed by western imperialist power. Freudian anthropology thus replicates a vulgar facsimile of 'double consciousness' for the western bourgeois psyche to experience as a

---

[113] W.E.B. DuBois, *The Souls of Black Folk*, (New York: Penguin Classics, 1903, 1994) p.5.

"decisive step towards a new orientation in the world and in science".[114]

In both instances, the normative gaze of established power overdetermines consciousness in a concerted attempt to subjugate our situated consciousness into 'objecthood', thus pacifying human agency into a harmonious accommodation with the imperial mainstream of modernity. Yet while Black subjectivity grows through dialectical resistance to modes of overdetermination-from-without imposed upon human 'being' by western imperialist power, western bourgeois subjectivity is socially consolidated by embracing modes of overdetermination-from-without introduced through hegemonic influence as a therapeutic validation of universal standards of human 'being'.[115]

Hence, the epistemological weight and socio-ontological implications of Freudian psychoanalytic theory must be thoroughly examined, even in the face of any alleged therapeutic relevance towards acclimatizing an 'empirical self-as-rational animality' towards normal functioning within an imperial

---

[114] Freud, *A General Introduction to Psychoanalysis*, (New York: Pocket Book, 1924, 1975) p.26.

[115] "There or here, it's the same thing: Oedipus is always colonization pursued by other means, it is the interior colony, and we shall see that even here at home, where we Europeans are concerned, it is our intimate colonial education." Gilles Deleuze and Felix Guattari, *Anti-Oedipus: Capitalism and Schizophrenia*, (New York: Penguin Books, 1972, 1977) p.170.

mainstream of modernity that structurally negates the assertion of Black subjectivity-as-human 'being'. This coercive anonymity, often masquerading as color blindness,[116] eliminates the possibility of epistemological neutrality with regards to the development of psychological categories, which purport to reveal, or provide the basis for, a universal human nature in concert with modernity. Such psychological categories, at best, provide tenuous guidelines for a specific socio-historically situated and biopolitically motivated imperial anthropology.

Therefore, critical interrogations of conceptions of Man implicated by reliance on psychoanalytic theory are vital precisely because the supposed epistemological gulf which distinguishes between psychological and socio-historical categories is merely a hegemonic illusion in the service of the normative gaze of Empire. "The traditional borderline between psychology on the one side and political and social philosophy on the other side have been made obsolete by the condition of man in the present era: formerly autonomous and identifiable psychical processes are being absorbed by the

---

[116] The oft stated disclaimer "I don't see people's skin color, I just see people", is basically a subtle rewording of the more accurate and racist statement: "I don't see people of your color as representative of what it means to be human, so please allow me to ignore the color of your skin so I can proceed to regard you as a normal person(colorless ie. White enough) and we can go on about our day without unnecessary incident".

function of the individual in the state – by his public existence".[117]

This supposed loss of autonomous subjectivity as indicative of the "condition of man in the present era", has been a structurally imposed socio-ontological condition long synonymous with the Real of lived Black experience, for which psychological categories have never existed within a vacuum outside the socio-political; nor have such psychological categories ever been immune to the currents of racist dehumanization inherent in modernity.[118] Therefore, questions involving psychological disorders are consistently inverted to correspond to the socio-historical conditions of lived Black experience and hence come into immediate confrontation with this "traditional borderline" of western imperialist power; a "borderline" that discursively frames our "public existence" as indicative of a restless, untamed and 'fixed' subhumanity that constitutes a 'problem' within modernity and thus a 'biopolitical danger' to a western imperialist continuum.

An imperial mainstream[119] emerged during modernity and ossified into a hyperreal simulation of

---

[117] Herbert Marcuse, *Eros and Civilization*, (Boston: Beacon Press, 1955, 1966) p.xxvii.

[118] Hussein Bulhan, *Frantz Fanon and the Psychology of Oppression*, (New York: Plenum Press, 1985).

[119] "Thus the masses are no longer simply those who are dominated, but rather the governed who are no longer in opposition, or whose opposition itself is integrated into the

itself with the onset of postmodernity, engulfing and overdetermining the nature of psychological independence experienced by an 'empirical self-as-rational animality', thus exemplifying the "condition of man in the present era". This phenomenon of imperialist 'ego' formation, as spiritual conformity to a hegemonic cauldron of mass agency constituted by the normative gaze of established power, funnels and transforms diverse potentialities of intersubjective resonance for genuine emancipatory community into consciousness more akin to a bewildered herd of rational animality. This is indicative of a tremendous psychological weight imposed by Empire upon the topographical coherence of mainstream subjectivity that consistently exhibits Bad Faith as self-deceiving moral ambivalence and ethical irresponsibility towards an ever present and anonymous structural-inert violence against human 'being'. An unremitting, unaccountable and therefore objective violence that severely impacts *the wretched of the earth* who constitute and are positioned as the socio-ontological underground of modernity.

---

positive whole, as a calculable and manipulable corrective that demands improvements in the apparatus. What was previously a political subject has become an object, and the antagonistic interests that were previously irreconcilable seem to have passed over into a true collective interest." Marcuse, *Five Lectures*, p.16.

Existential liberation critique provides an insurgent philosophical pivot from which to confront this "traditional borderline" between psychological and socio-historical orientations; namely through sociogenic[120] interrogations of psychoanalytic theory that critically behead the epistemological spectrum of phylogenetic[121] and ontogenetic[122] primacy regarding mental pathology as sheer irrelevance when faced with lived Black experience in relation to a western imperialist continuum. "Reacting against the constitutionalist tendency of the late nineteenth century, Freud insisted that the individual factor be taken into account through psychoanalysis. He substituted for the phylogenetic theory the ontogenetic perspective. It will be seen that the Black man's alienation is not an individual question. Beside phylogeny and ontogeny stands sociogeny."[123] Black subjectivity does not qualitatively suffer from undifferentiated psychological pathologies afflicting the

---

[120] Sociogenic refers to "explanations that are attuned to the social origins of human problems." Gordon, "The Black and The Body Politic: Fanon's Existential Phenomenological Critique of Psychoanalysis", included in *Fanon: A Critical Reader*, p.77.

[121] Regarding the Freudian conception of Man, Phylogenetic refers to "the growth of repressive civilization from the primal horde to the fully constituted civilized state". Marcuse, *Eros and Civilization*, p.20.

[122] Within a Freudian anthropological context, Ontogenic refers to "the growth of the repressed individual from early infancy to his conscious societal existence". Ibid.

[123] Fanon, *Black Skin, White Masks*, p.11.

western bourgeois 'empirical self-as-rational animality', for in relation to the normative gaze of modernity, Black subjectivity, as a corrosive wellspring
of socio-ontological pathology, is rendered incom-
mensurate with human 'being', therefore threatening to destabilize imperialist structures of meaning
that uphold western bourgeois subjectivity as universal human nature incarnate.

As such, "psychoanalysis cannot be deployed as
pure speculative knowledge or as a general theory
of man",[124] for once severed from its corpus of
western bourgeois subjectivity, the tumbling godhead of Freudian anthropology finds itself exposed
as socio-ontologically frail and epistemologically
wanting. "The governing rules of logic carry no
weight in the unconscious; it might be called the
Realm of the Illogical. Urges with contrary aims
exist side by side in the unconscious without any
need arising for an adjustment between them.
Either they have no influence whatever on each
other, or, if they have no decision is reached, but a
compromise comes about which is nonsensical since
it embraces mutually incompatible details. With
this is connected the fact that contraries are not kept
apart but treated as though they were identical, so
that in the manifest dream any element may also

---

[124] Foucault, *The Order of Things*, p.376.

have the meaning of its opposite."[125] What kind of conception of Man is ultimately reliant on such a "new orientation" regarded as a "decisive step towards a new orientation in the world and in science",[126] and for whom? And how does this "new" anthropological "orientation" relate to a western imperialist continuum?

Indeed, the Freudian turn functions as a "decisive step" towards reconstituting templates of Man-as-western bourgeois subjectivity. Hence, serviceably relegating consciousness of oppressive historical relations, that enshrine coloniality upon human

---

[125] Freud, *An Outline of Psycho-Analysis*, p.43. Sartre's critique is unsparing: "Thus I would reproach psychoanalytic theory with being syncretic and not dialectic thought. The word 'complex', indeed, indicates this very evidently: interpenetration without contradiction. I agree, of course that there may exist an enormous number of 'larval' contradictions within individuals, which are often translated in certain situations by interpenetrations and not by confrontations. But this does not mean these contradictions do not exist. The results of syncretism, on the contrary, can be seen in the idea of the Oedipus complex, for instance: the fact is that analysts manage to find everything in it, equally well the fixation on the mother, love of the mother, or hatred of the mother, as Melanie Klein argues. In other words, anything can be derived from it, since it is not structured. The consequence is that an analyst can say one thing and then the contrary immediately afterwards, without in any way worrying about a lack of logic, since after all 'opposites interpenetrate'. A phenomenon can mean this, while its contrary can also mean the same thing. Psychoanalytic theory is thus a 'soft' thought. It has no dialectical logic to it." Sartre, *Between Existentialism and Marxism*, (New York: Pantheon, 1972, 1974) p.38.
[126] Freud, *A General Introduction to Psychoanalysis*, p.26.

'being', to a vacuous psychological no man's land, a social 'id', or more aptly put; a collective unconscious[127] wherein Black people dwell in a dehumanized paradise of sterile phobogenic 'objecthood'.[128] The normative gaze of a western imperialist continuum posits that "the Negro has one function: that of symbolizing the lower emotions, the baser inclinations, the dark side of the soul",[129] thus subsuming our human 'being' within a coercive anonymity. As such, Black subjectivity that abdicates its constitutive self-determination to the normative gaze suffers a more pronounced intensification of 'double consciousness' under the weight of Freudian anthropology, thus provoking a hyper-reflexive overdetermination-from-without that seeks to acclimate the relentless transcendence and spiritual upheaval of our situated consciousness to the sover-

---

[127] "The collective unconscious is not dependent on cerebral heredity; it is the result of what I shall call the unreflected imposition of a culture." Fanon, p.191.

[128] "The choice of the phobic object is therefore overdetermined. This object does not come at random out of the void of nothingness; in some situation it has previously evoked an affect in the patient. His phobia is the latent presence of this affect at the root of his world; there is an organization which has been given a form. . . . In the phobic, affect has a priority that defies all rational thinking. As we can see, the phobic is a person who is governed by the laws of rational prelogic and affective prelogic: methods of thinking and feeling at which he experienced the event that impaired his security." Fanon, p.155.

[129] Fanon, p.190.

eign legitimacy of Empire by way of materialist mythology.

And therein modernity exhibits a reciprocal epistemological reliance on the mythologies of 'race' and 'the unconscious', sanctioning a conception of Man-as-western bourgeois subjectivity through Freudian anthropology that diffuses the exceptional antagonism disclosed by the assertion of Black subjectivity-as-human 'being' into instinctual conflicts and conventional psychological paradigms of neurosis and psychosis, thus disavowing the Raw coloniality of lived Black experience. As such, "enlightenment returns to mythology which it never really knew how to elude"[130] by disclosing a spiritually impoverished anthropology that socio-ontologically functions as a constitutive influence towards an 'empirical self-as-rational animality', a 'fixed' conception of Man which acquiesces to and accompanies western imperialist power.

The novel potentialities of existential liberationist critique, as witnessed in Fanonist and Sartrean interrogations of Freudian psychoanalysis, are paralleled in certain Freudo-Marxist trends within the Frankfurt School's project of critical theory. Marcuse for example, while in the process of recuperating the relevance of Freud's body of work into his

---

[130] Theodor Adorno and Max Horkheimer, *Dialectic of Enlightenment*, (New York: Herder and Herder, 1944, 1972) p.27.

own critique, is compelled in true existential liberationist fashion to conduct a sociogenic beheading of
his own; conceding that although Freudian theory
"appears to be purely biological", it's actually
"fundamentally social and historical".[131]   Indeed,
how could it be otherwise for a critical tradition
which has been so successful in theoretically trans-
planting a Marxist godhead upon Freud's corpus to
such a lasting effect? And although the discursive
stitching which binds this fusion can at times
loosen, become undone and be a bit biologically
determinist and unsightly in retrospect, it can still
critically function, even if somewhat ungainly so; as
clearly evidenced during the transition of this
Freudo-Marxist fusion away from an invigorating
source of critical theory[132] and towards its eventual
collapse into poststructuralist dogma.[133]

---

[131] Marcuse, *Five Lectures*, p.1.

[132] The Frankfurt School's inspired use of psychoanalytic theory
to critique fascism notwithstanding, perhaps this Freudo-Marxist
fusion simultaneously peaked and was exhausted with the
publication of *Anti-Oedipus: Capitalism and Schizophrenia* by
Gilles Deleuze and Felix Guattari?

[133] "All that blew away after 1970 with all the business about
desire and revolution and the mixing of the two . . . Some saw an
extreme radicalism in that. But the mix sounded the death-knell
of both desire and revolution. The blending of the two led to each
being neutralized by the other. There are many who based
themselves on this idea for a long time. . . . A whole generation
based themselves on this terrible ambiguity, on things that had, to
all intents and purposes, already disappeared. . . . The political
and libidinal dimensions lose their singularity. It was their

An existential liberationist critique of Freudian psychoanalysis severs the godhead of western bourgeois subjectivity from the body of Freud's work. Yet even more fundamentally, this sociogenic guillotine cuts to the core of modernity itself, challenging the onus of biological determinism that allows Freud's psychoanalytic anthropology to manifest itself as not only a historical possibility, but as a constitutive socio-ontological necessity which incarnates within each 'empirical self' a predisposition towards western imperialist domination as natural and ahistorical. Against Foucault, this is the Real of Freudian anthropology, the lived "relation of psychoanalysis with what makes all knowledge in general possible in the sphere of the human sciences."[134]

As Marcuse keenly and prophetically intimated, when seen from a Marxist orientation that privileges objective geopolitical and economic conditions, tracing their postmodern mutation into an expansive globalization of advanced neo-liberal capitalism, the Freudian conception of Man appears to be well on its way towards obsolescence, vanishing ever so slowly from its socio-historical primacy.[135]

---

singularity alone that gave them force. To mix the two was to contravene their irreducibility. It was after all, one hell of a misappropriation of Marx and Freud." Baudrillard, *Fragments*, (New York: Routledge, 2001, 2004) p.18.
[134] Michel Foucault, *The Order of Things*, p.376.
[135] "What are the historical changes that have made this conception obsolete? According to Freud, the fatal conflict

A Foucauldian reading however, all too easily dismisses the very possibility of a psychoanalytic anthropology as pious longing,[136] even while adamantly refusing to relinquish a theoretical methodology which would have been an impossibility without the very notion of an 'unconscious'; that fundamental pillar which constitutes Freudian anthropology itself. This epistemological parlor trick of dissolving Man, while making full use of theoretical gains that are born of adherence to a specific

---

between the individual and society is first and foremost experienced and fought out in the confrontation with the father: here, the universal struggle between Eros and Thanatos erupts and determines the development of the individual. And it is the father who enforces the subordination of the pleasure principle to the reality principle; rebellion and the attainment of maturity are stages in the contest of the father. Thus, the primary 'socialization' of the individual is the work of the family, as is whatever autonomy the child may achieve – his entire ego develops in a circle and refuge of privacy: becoming oneself with but also *against* the other. The 'individual' himself is the living process of *mediation* in which all the repression and liberty are 'internalized,' made the individual's own doing and undoing. Now, in this situation, in which the ego and superego were formed in the struggle with the father as the paradigmatic representative of the reality principle – this situation is historical: it came to an end with the changes in industrial society which took shape in the inter-war period. I enumerate some of the familiar features: transition from free to organized competition, concentration of power in the hands of an omnipresent technical, cultural and political administration, self-propelling mass production and consumption, subjection of previously private, asocial dimensions of existence to methodical indoctrination, manipulation, control." Marcuse, *Five Lectures*, p.46.
[136] Michel Foucault, p.379.

historically situated anthropology, only serves to collude with western imperialist power by reducing the socio-ontological significance of the murder of Man. This ill-fated Foucauldian insistence on the dissolution of Man has been co-opted and transformed into an annoying poststructuralist whine, which merely obfuscates the symbiotic relations between psychoanalytic anthropology, western bourgeois subjectivity, racist dehumanization and coloniality.

Fanon's sociogenic critique, when coupled with Sartre's virulent philosophical demolition of the 'unconscious'[137], provides the discursive rhythm for an existential liberationist confrontation of Freud that refuses to ignore the exceptional antagonistic disequilibrium introduced into a western imperial-

---

[137] "If we reject the language and the materialistic mythology of psychoanalysis, we perceive that the censor in order to apply its activity with discernment must know what it is repressing. In fact if we abandon all the metaphors representing the repression as the impact of blind forces, we are compelled to admit that the censor must choose and in order to choose must be aware of so doing. How could it happen otherwise that the censor allows lawful sexual impulses to pass through, that it permits needs (hunger, thirst, sleep) to be expressed in clear consciousness? And how are we to explain that it can relax its surveillance, that it can even be deceived by the disguises of the instinct? But it is not sufficient that it discern the condemned drives; it must also apprehend them as *to be repressed*, which implies in it at the very least an awareness of its activity. In a word, how could the censor discern the impulses needing to be repressed without being conscious of discerning them? How can we conceive of a knowledge which is ignorant of itself?" Sartre, *Being and Nothingness*, p.93.

ist continuum by the assertion of Black subjectivity-as-human 'being'. Tested against the edge of such an insurgent philosophical *tour de force*, Freudian anthropology is beheaded, just a wandering therapeutic corpse waiting for just enough of a critical push to collapse and double over itself. And yet, this triumph is short lived, for the Freudian conception of Man remains on its feet, a pyrrhic clone and defiantly headless apparition, destined to keep discursively treading on and on, for as long as possible; parasitically feeding off a western imperialist continuum from which it ultimately derives its epistemological sustenance and geohistorical relevance.

As an exceptional antagonism, the assertion of Black subjectivity-as-human 'being' against the normative gaze of western imperialist power allows for a constant renewal of penetrating awareness into the human condition; providing a vital rugged counter narrative of ascendant humanity against a sanitized historically polished progressive western imperialist narrative of modernity as universally emancipatory. The phenomenon of lived Black experience reveals an inherent totality of dehumanization affecting a vast range of humanity, even as it is rationally masked in racial categories which focus the effects of generalized oppression onto particular populations comprising the socio-ontological underground of modernity.[138]   As such, fundamental aspects of human 'being', overlooked, forgotten, misappropriated, and necessarily avoided by Man-as-western bourgeois subjectivity, are disclosed in the Raw coloniality of lived Black experience.

With mass incarceration of ascendant humanity as the lowest common denominator of 'the freest nation on earth', and the rampant unrepentant accumulative slaughter of youth at the hands of neo-colonial police entrusted to uphold 'law and order', to assert Black subjectivity-as-human 'being' intimately beckons a dread of familiarity with the fragile historical boundaries of human freedom, and the fleeting worldly dance of human mortality.   The Raw coloniality of lived Black experience goes unheeded at great risk to any relevant movement to confront Empire with emancipatory praxis.

Contemporary reconfigurations of Empire-as-western imperialist power indicate the prevalence of totalitarian security culture and economic austerity measures that are significantly furthering an already ongoing slow socio-cultural erosion of objective historical conditions[139] that provide an auth-

---

[138] This point is illustrated diligently and thoroughly by Reginald Major in his seminal work on the theory and history of the Black Panther Party, *A Panther is a Black Cat,* (Baltimore: Black Classics Press, 1971, 2006).

[139] "Some of the basic assumptions of Freudian theory both in their orthodox as well as revisionist development have become obsolescent to the degree which their object, namely, the

entic impetus towards the possibility of Man-as-western bourgeois subjectivity, even as the necessity for western bourgeois subjectivity has never been more ideologically imperative as a new 'cosmopolitan' incentive from which to justify the continuing spread of advanced neo-liberal capitalist globalization. And it is this conception of Man-as-western bourgeois subjectivity upon which any claim of the supposed universality of Freudian psychoanalysis rests.

This objective historical vacuity, coupled with the overriding ideological need for a globalized socio-ontological reinvestment back into the imperial mainstream, provides an impetus for the rise of a hyperbourgeois consciousness which is experienced as a blind refusal to relinquish the permanent appearance of western bourgeois subjectivity as natural and universal. This hyper-bourgeois subjectivity, at times even masquerading as 'cosmopolitanism',[140] is

---

'individual' as the embodiment of id, ego and superego has become obsolescent in the social reality. The evolution of contemporary society has replaced the Freudian model by a social atom whose mental structure no longer exhibits the qualities attributed by Freud to the psychoanalytic object. Psychoanalysis, in its various schools, has continued and spread over large sections of society, but with a change in its object, the gap between theory and therapy has been widened. Therapy is faced with a situation in which it seems to help the Establishment rather than the individual." Marcuse, *Five Lectures*, p.44.

[140] Kwame Anthony Appiah, *Cosmopolitanism: Ethics in a World of Stangers*, (New York: W.W. Norton & Company, 2006) and

a conscious postmodern attempt at openly over-compensating for the blood-letting universal pre-tense of classic bourgeois subjectivity, by opposing it with a simulacrum derived from the same wells-pring of imperialist epistemology.

Ontologically sedentary, classic bourgeois sub-jectivity approaches Freudian psychoanalysis with a serious temperament; as a constitutive tool for the development of a well-adjusted 'empirical self-as-rational animality', in dire need of psychological reinforcement to complement its already violently established socio-historical certitude. Hyperbour-geois subjectivity however, existentially aware of its lack of emancipatory integrity and moral legiti-macy, approaches psychoanalysis with an ironic temperament; as a consumer in dire need of socio-ontological security and the cultural recognition which comes from appropriating an established brand name; psychologically purchasing Freudian anthropology as a constitutive logo to loudly and publicly proclaim an affinity with a particular fashion of 'being-in-the-world'.

Although Marcuse claims that, "Freud's theory comprehended the past, rather than the present – a vanishing rather than a prevalent image of man, a

---

Jacques Derrida, *On Cosmopolitanism and Forgiveness*, (London: Routledge, 2001) are interesting examples.

disappearing form of human existence",[141] Man-as-western bourgeois subjectivity has never been much more than a mere "vanishing" act, whenever geo-historically faced with the socio-ontological demands of authentic human liberation. Indeed, "when I search for Man in the technique and style of Europe, I see only a succession of negations of man and an avalanche of murders."[142] Is not the celebrated Foucauldian dissolution of Man a petty and vulgar discursive reflection of this "succession of negations of man" back upon itself? And thus, revealing an epistemological escape route absolving Man of res-ponsibility for having committed "an avalanche of murders" by lessening its geohistorical relevance and socio-ontological intensity as a particularly con-stituted anthropology in direct correlation to a west-ern imperialist continuum.

Psychoanalytic theory justifies a continual structural-inert intrusion of this "succession of neg-ations" upon lived Black experience as "Man in the technique and style of Europe", arrogating poten-tialities of human agency by rationing out spiritual death in the guise of a harmonious assimilation into the imperial mainstream of modernity. Hence any claim suggesting the gradual disappearance of the Freudian conception of Man, existentially resonates

---

[141] Marcuse, p.45.
[142] Fanon, *The Wretched of the Earth*, p.312.

amongst those who recognize the tacit complicity between Freudian anthropology and the normative gaze of modernity.

Surprisingly, in this Marcuse erred fundamentally by attempting to recuperate an original Freudian anthropology which he regarded as "not only a past left behind, but a future to be recaptured"[143] against the tide of advanced neo-liberal capitalism. This philosophical blunder is common within oppositional orientations that differ from Marcuse's, in that their emancipatory project is exclusively anchored to the working class of the imperial mainstream, in effect, epistemologically appropriating the topographical coherence of a western imperialist continuum towards a political and socio-economic redemption of Empire, rather than Overturning coloniality through emancipatory praxis towards lived unity-as-diversity of authentic egalitarian geonational community.

Psychoanalytic theory still functions as an epistemological hygiene for western imperialist power, discursively cleansing a conception of Man-as-western bourgeois subjectivity that is underwritten by an "avalanche of murders", and thus reifying the negation of Black subjectivity-as-human 'being' within a stifling 'objecthood' and rational signification of subhumanity called 'race'. "The disaster of the

---

[143] Marcuse, p.61.

man of color lies in the fact that he was enslaved. The disaster and inhumanity of the white man lies in the fact that somewhere he has murdered Man."[144]

The biopolitical alterity of 'race' organizes humanity into a coherent topography of coloniality between imperial mainstream and socio-ontological underground of modernity, all the while fracturing potentialities of egalitarian human community through rational adherence to a mythic materialist determinism. A debasing materialist determinism that permeates modernity and is the very condition of possibility for both the fact of 'race', and the fact of a Freudian 'unconscious': two constitutive 'facts' of modernity which under close scrutiny reveal themselves as nothing more than two potent myths in ideological service to the normative gaze of a western imperialist continuum. "Psychoanalysis and ethnology occupy a privileged position in our knowledge – not because they have established the foundations of their positivity better than any other human science, and at last accomplished the old attempt to be truly scientific; but rather because, on the confines of all the branches of knowledge investigating man, they form an inexhaustible treasure-hoard of experiences and concepts, and above all a

---

[144] Fanon, *Black Skin, White Masks*, p.231. modified translation and capitalization my own.

perpetual principle of dissatisfaction, of calling into question, of criticism and contestation of what may seem, in other respects to be established. Now, there is a reason for this that concerns the object they respectively give to one another, but concerns even more the position they occupy and the function they perform within the general space of the *episteme*."[145]

As a discursive offspring of modernity, both the 'unconscious' and 'race' have no epistemological authority outside of a western imperialist continuum. This epistemological reliance ontologically limits the scope of their social application and existential relevance when confronted by the assertion of Black subjectivity-as-human 'being' as an exceptional antagonism that ultimately undermines imperialist structures of meaning. "Psychology could be elaborated and practical as a special discipline as long as the psyche could sustain itself against the public power, as long as privacy was real, really desired and self-shaped; if the individual has neither the ability neither the possibility to be for himself, the terms of psychology become the terms for societal forces which define the psyche."[146]

Therefore, the psychoanalytic conception of Man-as-western bourgeois subjectivity acculturates the

[145] Foucault, p.374.
[146] Marcuse, *Eros and Civilization*, p.xxvii.

biologically determinist proposition of an 'empirical self' as a pragmatic self-deceptive locus of rational animality, binding a myriad of justifications necessitating the abdication of human subjectivity towards achieving a lasting symmetry within the normative gaze of Empire. And thus, the assertion of Black subjectivity-as-human 'being' constitutes an exceptional antagonism towards "societal forces which define the psyche", introducing socio-ontological disequilibrium that hastens the "ability" for constitutive self-determination, relentless transcendence and spiritual upheaval, as an authentic "possibility" of situated consciousness.

The geohistorical praxis of western imperialist power is simultaneous with its biopolitical triumph as the anthropological standard bearer of human 'being'. Hence, the poststructuralist insistence on the dissolution of Man discursively absolves those who "never cease to talk of Man yet murder him on every street corner of the world",[147] by obfuscating the coherence of an imperial topography which divides mainstream from socio-ontological underground of modernity.

Freudian anthropology is epistemologically reliant on the universal permanence of a mechanistic and determinist conception of human nature which endorses "men who clearly do not find it easy to do

---

[147] Fanon, *The Wretched of the Earth*, p.314.

without satisfaction of this tendency to aggression that is in them" as a biological 'fact' of modernity. Freud claims that "when deprived of satisfaction of it they are ill at ease" and that "there is an advantage, not to be undervalued, in the existence of smaller communities, through which the aggressive instinct can find an outlet in enmity towards those outside the group". Freud even graciously elaborates that it "is always possible to unite considerable numbers of men in love towards one another, so long as there are still some remaining as objects for aggressive manifestations."[148]

Indeed, for *the wretched of the earth* populating the socio-ontological underground, precisely designated and overdetermined-from-without as exactly such subhuman "objects for aggressive manifestations", psychoanalytic theory tremendously fails to account for the irreducibility of our human agency as situated consciousness, epistemologically reprimanding spiritual autonomy with a distinctly Freudian anthropology.

As such, this Freudian conception of Man, which necessitates the formulation of a deterministic 'unconscious', has been little more than a vast canopy under which the psychological burden and socio-ontological residue of any inhumane, barbarous or savage act could dwell, without Man-as-

---

[148] Freud, *Civilization and its Discontents*, p.64.

western bourgeois subjectivity ever having to
confront existential responsibility and geohistorical
consequence. "All the knowledge within which
Western culture had given itself in one century
around a certain image of man, pivots on the work
of Freud, though without, for all that, leaving its
fundamental arrangement."[149]

Freudian anthropology grafts and upholds a
"strange representation" of "rigorous mechanistic
determinisms"[150] that promote and endorse a specific socio-historically situated formulation of human
subjectivity that not only creates the possibility of a
lie without a liar, but also racism without a racist,
and ultimately the murder of Man without a murd-
erer.

However, Freudian anthropology is no mere
anomaly, the beheading of which will cleanse and
redeem an epistemological orientation that aids and
abets the murder of Man. For even as Freudian
anthropology finds itself at the mercy of existential
liberation critique, in truth, the imperial mainstream
itself remains aloof and in Freud's psychological
debt, miseducated and coerced into continually suffering through a condition of spiritual poverty that
blindly shoulders the geohistorical brunt of a socio-
ontological pressure created by such a staunch

[149] Foucault, p.361.
[150] Jean-Paul Sartre, *Between Existentialism and Marxism*, p.37.

biopolitical allegiance to Man-as-western bourgeois subjectivity.

Thus, bereft of any hyperbourgeois sentimentality for a neurobiologically 'fixed' conception of Man as a sedentary deterministic puppet of the 'unconscious', and even amidst the growing discursive chorus of boisterous epistemological misgivings originating from Lacanian acolytes everywhere, whose poststructuralist clamor is indicative of a misguided attempt at an authentic returning to Freudian anthropology: off with the muth@f*ckin' head. Indeed, lest we ever forget, "the discoveries of Freud are of no use to us here"[151] in the underground of modernity.

---

[151] Fanon, *Black Skin, White Masks*, p.104.

rational animality versus ascendant humanity – Rational animality reifies the subordination of human agency to a mechanistic determinism of biological drives and neurological impulses completely bereft of constitutive agency and existential responsibility. Thus exercising freedom as sedentary 'being-in-the-world', closed off from potentialities of historical intervention within a constellation of imperialist structures of meaning, welcoming overdetermination-from-without upon situated consciousness, allowing for interpretations of structural-inert global power as the culmination of 'natural' evolutionary processes, and therefore historically invulnerable to any socio-ontological insurgency arising from the underground of modernity through emancipatory praxis.

Ascendant humanity actualizes constitutive freedom and existential responsibility as kinetic distance of situated consciousness, that lived rhythm of relentless transcendence and spiritual upheaval as irreducible cipher of human 'being', by exercising agency against hegemonic structures of meaning that bestow upon western imperialist power a mythology of perceived universal permanence meant to compromise the tireless dialectic mediation of emancipatory praxis upon history.

Trayvon Martin, biopolitical murder and Empire – The murder of Trayvon Martin reveals the extent of George Zimmerman's complete interiorization of the normative gaze of modernity. A normative gaze that intimately gestates as alienation from human 'being' within imperialist formations of identity, thus demeaning potentialities of intersubjective resonance towards a permanence of racist alterity between an anthropologically sanctioned 'being-in-the-world' constituted as the imperial mainstream, and a 'problematic' and biopolitically dangerous 'being-in-the-world' constituted as the socio-ontological underground of modernity. Zimmerman, not exactly one to ever be mistaken for belonging to the ruling power elite, is a working class collaborationist with Empire. As such, his racism vacillates between stages of objective and affective polarity, culminating in attempts at securing official sanction from Empire for his claim to mainstream identity through the biopolitical murder of Trayvon Martin.

Zimmerman patrols the imperially coherent topographical margins between mainstream and underground of modernity as an unpaid volunteer seeking socio-ontological security as an unofficial lackey of established power, without even the structural-inert legitimacy of neo-colonial police force to constitute the hegemonic sovereignty of Empire through objective violence. Indeed, his actions reveal a spiritual evasion of freedom and responsibility as Bad Faith, in the hopes of assuming a 'fixed' identity of 'empirical self-as-rational animality' within the imperial mainstream in exchange for embracing his own overdetermination-from-without.

From the safe confines of his vehicle, Zimmerman, former captain of the 'neighborhood watch', affirms the normative gaze of established power and is initially able *to see* Martin as "a real suspicious guy"[152] *without being seen*. Thus, sealing off the human trajectory of lived Black experience within 'objecthood', through the discursive zoological indictment of a "black male" nonchalantly walking around wearing a hooded sweatshirt. However, the racist dehumanizing privilege enjoyed by Zimmerman of *seeing without being seen*,[153] is soon fundamentally called into question by the recognition of Martin that he is being stalked. "Now he's staring at me." Even this slight intersubjective resonance between them is enough to temporarily disrupt Zimmerman's harmonious assimilation of the normative gaze that is predicated upon the socio-ontological imposition of

---

[152] All ensuing transcribed quotations of George Zimmerman based on https://viewfroml2.com/2012/04/05/minute-by-minute-timeline-of-trayvon-martins-death/

[153] "the white man has enjoyed the privilege of seeing without being seen." Sartre, "Black Orpheus", included in *What is Literature? and Other Essays*, (Cambridge: Harvard University Press, 1948, 1988) p.291.

an imperial coherent topography remaining imperceptible by the Other-as-subhuman 'objecthood'.

Zimmerman's racism is voluntaristic, freeing itself from the safe confines of the structural-inert, and as such he experiences the loss of his anonymity as a menacing turn requiring self-justification before the intersubjective resonance generated by Martin's gaze of recognition that decisively intervenes against Zimmerman's reliance on the privilege of *seeing without being seen*. Therefore, *being seen* by Martin confers upon Zimmerman a socio-ontological insecurity that spiritually erodes the core of racist presuppositions he seeks to 'fix' his identity upon: for when the Other introduces potentialities of 'being-towards-one another', and does not subscribe to the biological determinism of materialist subhuman 'objecthood', imperial mainstream subjectivity finds itself confronted with fundamental potentialities of discontinuity and reacts with an originary dehumanizing violence which is the very condition of its possibility.

George Zimmerman aspires to ground his claim for socio-ontological recognition through greater subservient affinity with established power, and yet such a project is undermined by Trayvon Martin's assertion of Black subjectivity-as-human 'being', an assertion that introduces a disequilibrium transforming Zimmerman's initial anonymous gaze of racist alterity into an intersubjective resonance of antagonistic reciprocity. Martin therefore thwarts Zimmerman's attempts at imperialist legitimacy by refusing to recognize him as synonymous with the objective violence of neo-colonial police force. In the absence of Martin's recognition of Zimmerman's attempt at imperialist self-deputization, Zimmerman threatens to impose his biopolitical alignment with Empire through intersubjective violence. Martin vehemently resists Zimmerman, as such, deciding to risk his life asserting Black subjectivity-as-human 'being' and is shot dead.

Righteous human outrage at the biopolitical murder of Trayvon Martin at the hands of George Zimmerman should not be confused with, or mediated by, the self-righteous chorus of 'liberal democratic' hyperbourgeois embarrassment over a 'not guilty' verdict that openly and unapologetically reconfirms the normative gaze of Empire regarding the assertion of Black subjectivity-as-human 'being' as a 'biopolitical danger'.

Legally sanctioning George Zimmerman's murder of Trayvon Martin, aside from granting social legitimacy to Zimmerman's project of seeking ontological self-validation from the topographical coherence of western imperialist power, actually works in tandem with media Spectacle towards reinvigorating American culture through barbaric random lynching as praxis that cements and transforms a general public into a racially partisan constituency. Such revivalist American constituency is indicative of a renewed threat to Black community by mainstream citizens of Empire, exercising a savage ethics of imperialist 'white' subjectivity-as-mob hegemony through ritualistic unexceptional oppressive violence when confronted by the assertion of Black subjectivity-as-human 'being'.

This renewed threat is immediately compounded by the already ominous structural-inert violence of ongoing neo-colonial police repression of human 'being'. For the assertion of Black subjectivity-as-human 'being' is consistently met with epistemeological skepticism and socio-historical brutality intent on suffocating the Promethean soul of an ascendant humanity. For if not kept intellectually docile through imperial mainstream assimilationist ideology, or physically incarcerated by a vast and ever-expanding prison industrial complex, Black community throughout the Diaspora constitutes a Trojan Horse[154] of lived potentialities for geonational insurrection-for-itself against Empire.

The normative gaze of western imperialist power divests structural-inert violence from its coercive

---

[154] "In this regard, Black Americans have a big role to play. They are a Black Trojan Horse within white America", Eldridge Cleaver, *Soul on Ice*, (New York: Delta/Dell Publishing, 1968, 1991) p.152.

anonymity upon its Return back to source as emancipatory praxis. As such, the original threat of oppressive violence by George Zimmerman against Trayvon Martin is completely indecipherable by the jury. This, in comparison to Trayvon's eman-cipatory exercise of human agency in resistance to such a threat, a response that in asserting Black subjectivity-as-human 'being' is immediately identi-fiable as illegitimate violence by jurists merely adhering to the 'law' as an exemplary legal codif-ication of the normative gaze.

Trayvon Martin's vociferous intersubjective res-istance against George Zimmerman's biopolitical encroachment upon his human 'being' profoundly disturbs the imperial mainstream sensibilities of the jurists. Indeed, such emancipatory human agency in resistance against a localized intersubjective man-ifestation of western imperialist power is still unfor-givable when embodied in Black subjectivity.

As an exceptional antagonism, lived Black exper-ience introduces geohistorical disequilibrium within the socio-ontological foundations of modernity. As such, for George Zimmerman or any other savage imbecile intent on nourishing racist reflexivity as an 'empirical self-as-rational animality' in constitutive subservience to globalized structural-inert power, there will always be a completely ethical and rational reason to shoot down those of us who, as

clearly and conveniently identified by the Raw coloniality of 'race', constitute an ever present 'biopolitical danger' to a western imperialist continuum. A
'biopolitical danger' that must be dealt with at all
costs: including an ongoing commitment to the
murder of Man as ultimate guarantee of an unjust
world order against any ascendant human initiative
exercised by *the wretched of the earth.*

Yearning, disaster and the Blues metaphysic - Yearning confronts the implicated temporality of human 'being' with lived potentialities as renunciation of conformity with the Real. Whereas desire voices satisfaction through consciousness experiencing attainment of tangible aims, Yearning enunciates a perpetually unattainable desire and intangible movement of consciousness towards the Divine.

Yearning thus overcomes situated limitations of base desire towards the Real, unveiling a pure intentionality of consciousness seeking realization as the tragedy of socio-ontological movement without possible fulfillment, the Blues metaphysic[155] of unrelenting crisis and struggle mediated through geohistorical transitions of ascent and descent anchored in disaster. "The disaster of the man of color lies in the fact that he was enslaved. The disaster and the inhumanity of the white man lie in the fact that somewhere he has murdered Man."[156]

The Blues metaphysic, as lived continuity of human suffering giving rise to an aesthetics sustaining Revolt against the disaster of coloniality in the Raw, unchains Yearning from demeaning itself as a restorative desire for absolute certitude mined from

---

[155] LeRoi Jones/Amiri Baraka, *Blues People*, (New York: William Morrow & Company, 1963). Angela Y. Davis, *Blues Legacies and Black Feminism*, (New York: Vintage, 1998).

[156] Fanon, *Black Skin, White Masks*, p.231. modified translation and capitalization my own.

a concrete mythological totality of a past that is irrevocably shattered, and from any literal prophetic expectancy for a future that will inevitably be decisively incomplete.

Shattering certitude in a fully constituted past, and dispelling hope for a comprehensively totalized future, discloses universality and releases lived potentialities for a poetic intentionality of human subjectivity from bondage to desiring acquiescence with the Real, thus introducing conditions for the possibility of a dialectic rhythm of lyrical consciousness and socio-ontological dissonance which resists the harmony of the normative gaze, transcends the legitimacy of established power and disrupts the equilibrium of a western imperialist continuum.

emancipatory aesthetics in the Raw – Defining Art as the manifest assertion of human creativity given form through freedom, intentionality and rigor of technique, brings within its scope all manner of artistic endeavor, while simultaneously confronting and undermining hierarchies of imperial coherence that privilege 'fine' over 'popular' art. To focus on aesthetics as a philosophical orientation engages Art in relation to perception, imagination and affective sensibility, while questioning established parameters of Truth and prevailing standards of Beauty. And yet, such philosophical engagement with aesthetic concerns, inevitably reveals an autonomous horizon for interrogations of consciousness and lived experience, thus inciting profound questions concerning human 'being'.

A considerable amount of literature and theory already exists in religious devotion to the importance of Art. This is no accident, for even as modernity loudly and structurally dispenses with any epistemological loyalty to outward religious truth; religious aims persist through the capacity of artistic endeavor to approach the Divine as imperatives beyond the base materiality of human needs, thereby disclosing a qualitative spiritual autonomy in resistance and transcendence of the Real.[157]

---

[157] "The relative autonomy of the developing Negro Christian religious gathering made it one of the only areas in the slave's life

Tremendous discursive efforts congest around ideological temperaments that posit some kind of obvious worth inherent to Art in and of itself, enshrining "the temptation of irresponsibility"[158] along with valuations of absolute truth and self-evident beauty around aesthetic principles that are necessarily and completely isolated from historical circumstance, social relevance, creative rigor and even the intentionality of the Artist.

It is precisely against such ideological tempera-ments of creative unaccountability and social irre-

---

where he was relatively free of the white man's domination. (Aside from the more formally religious activities of the fledgling Negro churches, they served as the only centers where the slave community could hold strictly social functions.) The 'praise nights,' or 'prayer meetings,' were also the only times when the Negro felt he could express himself freely and emotionally as possible. It is here that music becomes indispensable to any discussion of Afro-Christian religion." Leroi Jones/Amiri Baraka, *Blues People*, p.40.

"Art, since it became autonomous, has preserved the utopia that evaporated from religion." Max Horkheimer, *Critical Theory: Selected Essays*, (New York: Continuum, 1968, 1972) p.275.

"Indeed, any historical (or emotional) line of ascent in Black music leads us inevitably to religion, ie., spirit worship. This phenomenon is always at the root in Black art, the worship of spirit – or at least the summoning of or by such a force." Leroi Jones/Amiri Baraka, *Black Music*, (New York: Quill, 1967) p.181-2.

"Artworks detach themselves from the empirical world as if this other world too were an autonomous entity." Theodor W. Adorno, *Aesthetic Theory*, (Minneapolis: University of Minnesota Press, 1970, 1997) p.1.

[158] Sartre, "Introducing *Les Temps Modernes*", included in *What is Literature? and Other Essays*, p.249.

sponsibility, often festering in the imperial mainstream amongst hyperbourgeois adherents of 'arts
for art's sake', and in contrast to well-meaning part-
isans of social realism and spiritually complacent
purveyors of poststructuralist pretense, that the cultivation of emancipatory aesthetics is imperative.[159]

Emancipatory aesthetics poses questions of artistic theory and creative praxis from an existential
liberationist dialectic that consciously embraces an
unrelenting tension between human agency and
structural-inert global power that is altogether avoided by any suggested divorce of cultural criticism
from the Real. Artistic endeavor is drenched with
'being-in-the-world', for it "summons and describes
where its energies were gotten . . . But the
description is of a total environment. The content
speaks of this environment as does the form".[160]
Hence, emancipatory aesthetics provides a vital
gateway towards understanding socio-ontological
questions about the constitution of human subjectivity, particularly in so far as these questions might

---

[159] "Our espousal of art thus becomes no mere idle acceptance of
'art for art's sake,' or the cultivation of the last decades of the
over-civilized, but rather a deep realization of the fundamental
purpose of art and of its function as a tap root of vigorous,
flourishing living." Alain Locke, "Art or Propaganda?", *Harlem*,
Vol.1 (November, 1928). Included in *Voices from the Harlem
Renaissance*, Edited by Nathan Huggins, (Oxford: Oxford Univ.
Press, 1978, 1995) p.313.
[160] LeRoi Jones/Amiri Baraka, *Black Music*, p.186.

inform or contribute towards dynamic projects of human liberation.

Authentic works of Art exert a qualitative spiritual autonomy over established structures of meaning by simultaneously resisting and transcending the Real. "The aesthetic form constitutes the autonomy of art vis a vis 'the given.' However, this dissociation does not produce 'false consciousness' or mere illusion but rather a counterconsciousness: negation of the realistic-conformist mind."[161] Still, Art is inevitably influenced and mediated by socio-historical conditions that thoroughly implicate any artistic endeavor, this, in spite of the irreducibility of aesthetic horizon to the Real.

Art is emancipatory-as-resistance by indulging insurgent content that bestows an aesthetic weight that intersubjectively resonates explicitly against Empire. Art is emancipatory-as-transcendence by cultivating insurgent style through aesthetic form that pierces the normative gaze of established power thereby unsettling structures of meaning that have become saturated with oppression through acquiescence to a western imperialist continuum. Whenever these orientations of resistance and transcendence coincide in tense dynamic unity, the singular aesthetic gravity of a work of Art approx-

---

[161] Herbert Marcuse, *The Aesthetic Dimension*, (Boston: Beacon Press, 1978) p.8.

imates universal relevance and births immense emancipatory potentialities.

The aesthetic gravity between resistance and transcendence is the source of all authentically emancipatory Art. Yet the creative tension from this aesthetic gravity originates in that problematic yet fundamental current of artistic endeavor: a qualitative spiritual autonomy encompassing both aesthetic realization of the work of Art and aesthetic intentionality of the Artist. For as Wright forcefully elucidates, "the artist must bow to the monitor of his own imagination; must be led by the sovereignty of his own impressions and perceptions; must be guided by the tyranny of what troubles and concerns him personally; and that he must learn to trust the impulse, vague and compulsive as it may be, which moves him in the first instance toward expression. There is no other true path, and the artist owes it to himself and to those who live and breathe with him to render unto reality that which is reality's."[162] Thus, the emancipatory bearing of Art, as resistance and transcendence, diminishes when either aesthetic weight or aesthetic form appeases the normative gaze of Empire, thereby ultimately eroding the "sovereignty" of our own "perceptions".

---

[162] Richard Wright, "Letter to Alessandro Franconi – Nov. 1944", *Richard Wright Reader,* (New York: Da Capo Press, 1978, 1997) p.70-71.

Art's genesis via human subjectivity is inevitably mediated by the Real, and yet this in no way absolves the Artist of accountability from which there is no easy or decisive reconciliation. For the Artist lives out explicitly through creative endeavor, the anguish of choice, dread of agency, and burden of responsibility that implicitly inform the human condition shared by us all.[163]

Indeed, we are all situated within Empire, a heavily administered world of western imperialist power, permeated by the influences of concentrated capital, racist dehumanization as coloniality in the Raw, globalized neo-liberal austerity and indefinite militaristic expansion. Hence, there is no cultural logic independent of Empire, and each Artist is thus implicated by their lived relation to the global scope of established power. Indeed, the normative gaze of Empire constitutes and endorses anthropological standards of human 'being' that are unapologetically transmitted through cultural means (be it 'high' culture associated with a western imperialist continuum or 'popular' culture associated with the Blues metaphysic) that continually reach an ever-

---

[163] "Each age discovers an aspect of the human condition; in every era man chooses himself in confrontation with other individuals, love, death, the world: and when adversaries clash . . . it is that metaphysical choice, that singular and absolute project which is at stake." Sartre, "Introducing *Les Temps Modernes*", included in *What is Literature? and Other Essays*, p.254.

widening audience through global media expansion and burgeoning technological integration.

The ardent search for *a priori* universally authoritative aesthetic standards from which to comprehensively judge, create or appreciate works of Art is a quixotic adventure without end. For although aesthetic standards do exist in every creative field imaginable, the significance of their authority is merely contingent upon the ever tense relation between vested subjectivity and the normative gaze. Even supposedly hallowed standards, ideologically recycled from generation to generation, have no genuine aesthetic leverage from which to claim any binding universal authority, except in their sanctioned relation to established power. Such standards are often culturally mired in the aesthetic residue of dogma, tradition, and at times, even pure and deliberate mystification generated through an abiding loyalty to the normative gaze of a western imperialist continuum.

Therefore, an awareness of the culture industry[164] that binds aesthetics to Empire becomes paramount for piercing the normative gaze of a western imperialist continuum that constitutes, structures, and regulates the artistic potentialities of creative consciousness into an endless repetition of aesthetic

---

[164] Theodor Adorno and Max Horkheimer, *Dialectic of Enlightenment*, pp.120-167.

banality and socio-historical mendacity culminating in commodity-as-art enabled by the clone-as-artist.

With the advanced neo-liberal capitalist inversion of the commercialization of Art into positing pure commodity itself as Art, Empire effectively responds to a "critique of the culture industry" which "is no longer innovative but obvious",[165] thereby shifting ideological emphasis away from the need to concern itself with co-opting whatever residue of emancipatory potentialities remain among both elite and grassroots factions of the postmodern lumpenproletariat. This is achieved by endorsing a cultivated aesthetic laundering of commodity through culture that actually mirrors an even more brazen laundering of unregulated global capital through the Art world and culture industry.

For even the most blatantly commercialized works of Art may exhibit a capacity to perpetuate the unrelenting tension between human agency and the Real, necessarily invoking an aesthetic horizon of qualitative spiritual autonomy which mediates against its own deliberate exploitation; retaining just enough emancipatory potentialities to initiate an introduction of discontinuity within the normative gaze. However, commercial Art's inversion into commodity-as-art nullifies this tension, moving

---

[165] Antonio Negri, *Empire and Beyond*, (Cambridge: Polity Press, 2006, 2008) p.99.

towards closing the gap between aesthetic horizon and the Real. This aesthetic closure effectively seals off access to that qualitative spiritual autonomy of Art: rendering the gravity of resistance and transcendence inaudible and mute, a static banality wholly bereft of creative freedom, artistic intentionality and rigor of technique.

Empire, unsatisfied with an already pervasive commercialization of Art, imposes overdetermination-from-without upon artistic endeavor towards production of commodity-as-Art,[166] thus reaffirming a hierarchy positing aesthetic alterity of materialist consumption, over and above the compelling intersubjective resonance of aesthetic discourse. Commodity-as-Art adheres to a vulgar materialist collapse of the aesthetic horizon upon itself, militating against the trajectory of human 'being' towards the Divine that births human subjectivity, smugly content with an impasse of lived experience confronting the evident as existentially exhaustive.

The clone-as-artist, thoroughly lacking any creative intentionality outside of a "commercial strategy of nullity", has no artistic vision beyond the

---

[166] "Therein lies all the duplicity of contemporary art: asserting nullity, insignificance, meaninglessness, striving for nullity when already null and void. Striving for emptiness when already empty. Claiming superficiality in superficial terms." Jean Baudrillard, *The Conspiracy of Art*, (New York: Semiotext(e), 2005) p.27.

demands of the culture industry, has no authentic understanding of artistic rigor, and has absolutely no stake whatsoever in any genuine lived experience involved in creating works of Art.[167] Thus, the anaesthetization of artistic culture (both 'high' and 'popular') colludes with Empire to such a degree that it initiates a potent suffocation of emancipatory potentialities from artistic endeavor by "confiscating banality, waste and mediocrity as values and ideologies."[168] This usurpation of Art by banality-as-culture effectively eases the necessary tension between aesthetic horizon and the Real, thereby stifling access to a qualitative spiritual autonomy that fuels creative antagonisms between artistic endeavor and imperialist structures of meaning. Under such circumstances, contemporary Art colludes with the normative gaze of Empire by functioning as an ideological anaesthetic reveling in nullity "which means nothing and it none the less exists, providing itself with all the right reasons to exist. This paranoia in collusion with art means that there is no longer any possible critical judgment, and only an amiable, necessarily genial sharing of

---

[167] "Art now offers career benefits, rewarding investments, glorified consumer products just like any other corporation." Sylvere Lotringer, "The Piracy of Art", the introductory essay to Baudrillard's *The Conspiracy of Art*, p.11.
[168] Baudrillard, *The Conspiracy of Art*, p.27.

nullity."[169]   Even a brief perusal of the majority of contemporary cultural criticism reveals just how much this "genial sharing of nullity" is becoming an art form in and of itself.

The oppressive structural-inert violence which subsumes the socio-ontological underground of modernity, continuously Returns to source as insurrection-in-itself as seen explicitly in Los Angeles (1992), Paris (2005), and London (2011).   As such, these potent historical dynamics of spontaneous rebellion and protest-as-resistance underscore the persistence of emancipatory aesthetics cultivated through Hip Hop culture towards facilitating a shared unrepentant affirmation of human agency by postmodern lumpenproletariat subjectivity against Empire.[170]

This is not to suggest a causal or deterministic relation between Hip Hop culture and these specific outbreaks of socio-historical revolt.   Rather, emph-

---

[169] Baudrillard, p.28.

[170] "Ice Cube Reflects on How the LA Riots Changed Rap", Courtney Garcia, (thegrio.com), 4-29-2012.

"Uprising, Hip Hop and the LA Riots", VH1 Documentary which aired 9pm Tuesday night, 4-31-12.

"French Rap Musicians Blamed for Violence", Sylvia Poggioli, (NPR.org), 12-14-2005.

"Should Rap Take the Rap for Rioting", Joe Muggs, (telegraph.co.uk), 12-8-2005.

"London Riots: Is Rap Music to Blame for Encouraging this Culture of Violence?", Paul Routledge, (mirror.co.uk), 8-10-2011.

"The Riots, the Rappers and the Anglo-Jamaican tragedy", David Goodhart (prospectmagazine.co.uk), 8-17-2011.

asis must be placed on the creative influence of authentic Hip Hop aesthetics towards constituting and sustaining modes of rebellious human subjectivity that remain defiant against established power, cultivating lived cultural potentialities of insurrection-in-itself as the Return of oppressive structural-inert violence. This, even as Hip Hop culture currently finds itself on the receiving end of an advanced neo-liberal capitalist assault of commercialized attrition that ruthlessly exploits the chronic economic woe and "spiritual instability"[171] of its postmodern lumpenproletariat adherents.

The overwhelming effectiveness of this comercialized attrition has forced genuine Hip Hop culture back underground. However, it is precisely the global Hip Hop underground where emancipatory aesthetics thrive in the Raw of vigorous authentic Hip Hop praxis (B-Boying/breakdancing, Graffitti writing, rapping/eMCeeing, and DJing/beatmaking) that culturally encourages the overthrow of ideology which cements spiritual subservience to a western imperialist continuum, and intellectually enables radicalization of postmodern lumpenproletariat consciousness.[172] And it is this 'taking conscience' which then makes the postmodern lumpen-

---

[171] Fanon, *The Wretched of the Earth*, p.137.
[172] I explore postmodern lumpenproletariat subjectivity, intellectual engagement and Hip Hop aesthetics as cultural resistance in *Hip Hop Intellectual Resistance*, (Xlibris, 2009).

proletariat much more likely to 'set it off' and ignite genuine socio-historical upheaval through spontaneous rebellion and 'protest-as-resistance', as opposed to just mere 'protest-as-ritual event'.

Artistic endeavor that aims to mount a challenge to established structures of meaning must ultimately confront an uncertainty rooted in a lived tension generated by the exercise of creative freedom situated within the imperial mainstream-as-civil society. Tension arises because this exercise of creative freedom is indicative of a qualitative spiritual autonomy that does not necessitate the socio-historical transformation of globally pervasive structural-inert oppression as a condition of its realization.[173] However, it is precisely this qualitative spiritual autonomy from existing socio-historical conditions that ultimately allows Art to function as a vital cultural reservoir that houses, preserves and transmits insurgent potentialities of human 'being' against the normative gaze of Empire.

Art manifests gateways towards an aesthetic horizon in constant mediation of resistance and transcendence against the Real, disclosing entire

---

[173] "But what appears in art as remote from the praxis of change demands recognition as a necessary element in a future praxis of liberation . . . Art cannot change the world, but it can contribute to changing the consciousness and drives of the men and women who could change the world." Marcuse, *The Aesthetic Dimension*, pp.32-33.

constellations of consciousness, imagination, historical memory, and lived experience, from which to inform, refresh and inspire emancipatory praxis, or even sedate it. The distance existing between an aesthetic horizon preserving emancipatory potentialities, and the Raw of emancipatory praxis, is often exploited by established unjust global power as an end in and of itself, for the purpose of lucrative cultural commodification that ultimately reinforces the social stabilization of a western imperialist continuum. As such, "it is self-evident that nothing concerning art is self-evident anymore, not its inner life, not its relation to the world, not even its right to exist".[174] The severity of this statement is no less true, and actually even more pronounced for those of us who find ourselves in the socio-ontological underground of modernity by dint of the Raw coloniality of our 'race',[175] itself indicative of the 'biopolitical danger' our ascendant humanity poses to Empire.

---

[174] Adorno, *Aesthetic Theory*, p.1.
[175] "The Negro is intrinsically a colonial subject, but one who lives not in China, India or Africa but next door to his conquerors, attending their schools, fighting their wars, and laboring in their factories. . . the world's fate is symbolically prefigured in the race relations of America." Richard Wright, *Conversations with Richard Wright* edited by Keneth Kinnamon and Michel Fabre, (Jackson: University of Mississippi Press, 1947, 1993) p.125.

For if potentialities of composing lyric poetry[176] truly troubled Adorno only after the horrific rational imposition of coloniality on Europe by Nazi Germany,[177] how does one begin to comprehend the unproblematic, and uninterrupted composing of lyric poetry for generations throughout the inception of modernity and the barbaric rational imposition of coloniality upon the rest of the world? Is it not that "political falsehood stains the aesthetic form"?[178] Somehow, the initiating violence of western imperialist aggression doesn't register on the socio-onto-

---

[176] "I have no wish to soften the saying that to compose lyric poetry after Auschwitz is barbaric." Adorno, *Aesthetics and Politics*, (London: Verso, 1977, 2007) p.188.

[177] "There was no Nazi atrocity – concentration camps, wholesale maiming and murder, defilement of women or ghastly blasphemy of childhood – which the Christian civilization of Europe had not long been practicing against the colored folk in all parts of the world in the name of and for the defense of a Superior Race born to rule the world." W.E.B. DuBois, *The World and Africa*, (New York: International Publishers, 1946, 2007) p.23.

"Not long ago Nazism transformed the whole of Europe into a veritable colony." Fanon, p.137.

". . . that if he rails against him, he is being inconsistent and that, at bottom, what he cannot forgive Hitler for is not *crime* in itself, *the crime against man*, it is not *the humiliation of man as such*, it is the crime against the white man, the humiliation of the white man, and the fact that he applied to Europe colonialist procedures which until then had been reserved exclusively for the Arabs of Algeria, the coolies of India, and the blacks of Africa."

Aime Cesaire, *Discourse on Colonialism*, (New York: Monthly Review Press, 1955, 1972) p.14.

Sven Lindqvist, *"Exterminate All The Brutes"*, (New York: The New Press, 1992, 1996).

[178] Adorno, p.188.

logical Richter scale whenever "the abundance of real suffering" that "tolerates no forgetting"[179] is visited upon *the wretched of the earth*. The normative gaze ultimately recognizes unjustifiable violence as occurring only whenever Man-as-western bourgeois subjectivity is forced to stare down the wrong end of the barrel of a gun. This occurs often enough during internecine conflicts involving competing imperialist projects, or when oppressive violence Returns to source through modes of emancipatory praxis against Empire.

Empire is rooted in the peculiar epistemological ground of modernity, as ordered according to the socio-ontological precepts of a western imperialist continuum that envelops lived Black experience within a coercive anonymity rendering our human 'being' invisible, and hence unworthy of serious ethical or moral consideration before the normative gaze of structural-inert global power. As such, the assertion of Black subjectivity-as-human 'being' constitutes an exceptional antagonism of ascendant humanity indicative of a profound depth of socio-ontological upheaval against imperialist structures of meaning, thus manifesting a vast reservoir of emancipatory aesthetic potentialities through the Blues metaphysic. Indeed, as Marcuse understood, "a far more subversive universe of discourse ann-

---

[179] Adorno, p.189.

ounces itself in the language of the Black militants. Here is systematic linguistic rebellion which smashes the ideological context in which the words are employed and defined, and places them in the opposite context – negation of the established one".[180] It is thus no coincidence that in the aftermath of the obvious decimation of Black liberation praxis by Empire-as-western imperialist power, displaced insurgent Black discourse finds epistemological shelter within the aesthetic horizon of lived historical memory among the postmodern lumpenproletariat purveyors of Hip Hop culture.

The Blues metaphysic communicates the assertion of Black subjectivity-as-human 'being' against western imperialist power through artistic endeavor, an aesthetic persistence of exceptional antagonistic resonance exposing that fundamental socio-ontological fault line of modernity: racist dehumanization. The tremors of this racist dehumanization continually threaten to destabilize the relevance of aboveground opposition against Empire as mobilized under exclusively western emancipatory precepts, whenever that struggle is spiritually disengaged from underground insurgency that finds its epistemological epicenter wherever the universality of Man is extolled while the actual murder of

---

[180] Marcuse, *Essay on Liberation*, (Boston: Beacon Press, 1975) p.35.

human 'being' is a rational outcome of globalized structural-inert power.[181]

Empire deterritorializes "the colonial situation" as globalized coloniality through which any emancipatory aesthetic "dynamism" that awakens human subjectivity-as-lived universal is "replaced fairly quickly by a substantiation of the attitudes of the colonizing power. The area of culture is then marked off by fences and signposts."[182] These cultural "fences" and aesthetic "signposts" effectively quarantine emancipatory potentialities of human agency that resist being diluted into "the neutrality of the spectator",[183] continuously perpetuating imperialist structures of meaning.

Emancipatory potentialities thus remain quarantined within a prison of self, an 'empirical self-as-rational animality' through which human agency is reduced to a regimen of organizing our own passivity.[184] Hence, any claim of permanence or stability grounded in cultural identity as designated by the "signposts" of western imperialist power is socio-ontologically at odds with the relentless transcen-

---

[181] Fanon, p.311.
[182] Fanon, p.236.
[183] Adorno, p.180.
[184] "What kind of prison can be devised for the highly subversive forces of individual creativity? - The rulers last dance here is to turn us all into the organizers of our own passivity." Raul Vaneigem, *Revolution of Everyday Life*, (London: Rebel Press/Left Bank Books, 1967, 1994) p.192.

dence of our human 'being'. Advanced neo-liberal
capitalist globalization can thus effortlessly endorse
any culturally pluralistic claim of 'identity' without
reserve, for it is achieved at the expense of insurgent
imperatives for human subjectivity-as-lived universal which have been abdicated in favor of cloning a
plethora of colorful "aesthetic expressions of respect
for the established order", thus fostering a socio-
ontological "atmosphere of submission and of inhi-
bition which lightens the task of policing consider-
ably."[185]

This pervasive abdication of human subjectivity
cedes our irreducible agency of situated consciousness for an overdetermined 'empirical self-as-rational animality' in deference to the normative gaze of
a western imperialist continuum. As such, the
cultivation of emancipatory aesthetics awakens insurgent potentialities of genuine human subjectivity,
stimulating constitutive self-determination against
the confines of an imperial mainstream that ethic-
ally functions with intersubjective indifference and
historical immunity towards neo-colonial police
murder, accumulative slaughter, mass incarceration, immigration internment camps, "the continuous surveillance of populations, the labeling of
at-risk individuals, legalized torture, psychological
warfare, police control of Publicity, the social mani-

---

[185] Fanon, p.38.

pulation of affects", as a perpetual coloniality of "uninterrupted war, mostly carried on without a fuss"[186] against the socio-ontological underground.

The normative gaze of Empire overdetermines the ordinary experience of spiritually compliant non-resisting mainstream populations by "the total mobilzation of all media for the defense of established reality" and "has coordinated the means of expression to the point where communication of transcending contents becomes technically impossible".[187] This technical impossibility occurs when such "transcending contents" oppose advanced neo-liberal capitalist globalization on unreflective ahistorical terms of engagement, aesthetically replicating dehumanizing socio-ontological presuppositions of modernity, even while vociferously raising the clamor of 'protest-as-ritual event' against the latest oppressive symptom, effectively veiling ongoing reconfigurations of western imperialist power.

Contemporary artistic endeavor seeking emancipatory bearing in the face of Empire must overcome any tendency towards satisfaction with even the most explicit indictments of structural-inert global power. For no matter how thorough the condem-

---

[186] Tiqqun, *This is Not a Program*, (Los Angeles: Semiotext(e), 2009, 2011) p.92-93.
[187] Marcuse, *One Dimensional Man*, (Boston: Beacon Press, 1964, 1991) p.68.

nation, if Art fails to convey creative potentialities towards constituting new 'human subjectivity-as-lived universal', thus introducing genuine disequilibrium[188] within a western imperialist continuum, then it falls quite short of emancipatory aesthetics in the Raw.

For the Truth of human 'being', and the Beauty of tireless struggle for human liberation against Empire-as-western imperialist power, though loyal to artistic endeavor, is irreducible to aesthetic form.

---

[188] "Decolonization, which sets out to change the order of the world, is, obviously, a program of complete disorder." Fanon, p.36.

Eric Garner and the suffocation of human 'being' –
Empire is incomprehensible without a permanent
police presence enforcing coloniality; rational pursuit of racist dehumanization is the very condition
of its possibility. Mass incarceration, normalized
torture, immigrant internment camps, mass surveillance; systematic disregard of human 'being' is no
anomaly in relation to advanced neo-liberal capitalist society but the Real of western imperialist
power.

Structural-inert violence as embodied by neo-
colonial police force exists as such a commonly occurring regularity within western imperialist metropoles, that it objectively functions throughout modernity in utter anonymity. As such, this structural-
inert violence barely creates a social tremor and
does not violate the 'law', but rather invests the
'law' with a sovereign legitimacy that is decisively
called into question by an exceptional antagonism
arising from the socio-ontological underground of
modernity: the assertion of Black subjectivity-as-
human 'being'.

An unforgiving biopolitical alterity of coloniality
in the Raw becomes apparent in the ensuing confrontation between Empire and the assertion of
Black subjectivity-as-human 'being', as five neo-
colonial police agents surround Eric Garner, who
attempts to overcome this socio-ontological impasse
by pleading for some kind of human recognition

from these imperial state sanctioned assailants, regarding his consistent and unwarranted harassment:

"Every time you see me, you mess with me!"[189]

The police move closer and remain poised to act at any moment without ceding recognition of his humanity by responding too much, or genuinely acknowledging in the least, any of Garner's excited claims. These agents of neo-colonial 'law' enforcement do not actually *see* him. However, what they do *see* is a 'phobogenic object', a constant and recurring 'biopolitical danger' that threatens the peaceful and orderly maintenance of a western imperialist continuum.

Eric Garner's affective realization of his own socio-ontological anonymity, a lived experience of human 'being-in-the-world' without existential merit before the normative gaze of established power, when combined with the awareness of neo-colonial police edging slowly a bit closer and closer to him, transforms the futility of this discursive plea for recognition, into an adamant assertion of human agency, a naked refusal to adhere to the inevitable conclusion of his certain detention and possible arrest:

"I'm tired of it, this stops today!"

---

[189] All ensuing transcribed quotations of Eric Garner based on https://www.youtube.com/watch?v=JpGxagKOkv8 from *New York Daily News*.

Unfortunately, "this" doesn't stop, even after attempting to rally other people around him in support of his claims, hoping that such a rapid exercise of intersubjective resonance bearing witness on his behalf might somehow circumvent the encroaching socio-ontological tyranny of neo-colonial 'law' enforcement.

"Everybody standing here, they tell you I ain't do nothin'!"

The structural-inert violence of neo-colonial police agents is physically palpable enough to ensure that everybody remains standing there in a reified stupor, and no amount of discursive support from a gathering crowd prevents the murder of Man from taking place on yet another street corner of a world ordered according to the precepts of modernity as imposed by western imperialist power.

Media exposure of video footage, which captures the neo-colonial police murder of Eric Garner, temporarily breaks through the monotony of objective violence against human 'being' and yet ultimately transforms this routine operation into Spectacle, as that which, though indicative of an imperial coherence of topographical positionality, is posited as an excessive, extreme and singular phenomenon. The function of Spectacle displaces murder from the Real of its socio-historical roots and as such, distills genuine potentialities of emancipatory praxis into 'protest-as-ritual event'. However, it will take much more than such 'protest-as-ritual event', no matter how sincere in appealing to the democratic moral simulacra of an advanced neo-liberal capitalist society, to bring this oppression of human 'being' to an end. Racist dehumanizing structural-inert violence won't stop today, or tomorrow, until it dialectically Returns to source as a phenomenon of emancipatory praxis that simultaneously facilitates a socio-ontological rebirth of human subjectivity-as-lived universal.

Until the Return of objective violence to its constitutive genesis via emancipatory praxis however, any such lived potentialities of human subjectivity-as-lived universal, much like those introduced by Eric Garner's assertion of Black subjectivity-as-human 'being', experience the same fate as Garner himself, and suffocate to death under the chokehold of structural-inert oppression renewed by five neo-colonial police agents against Man.

"I can't . . . breathe."

"I . . . can't breathe."

"I . . . can't . . . breathe . . ."

insurrection-in-itself – The murder of human 'being' is no accident that can be corrected by proper legislation or civic oversight of neo-colonial police activity. Nor is such ongoing murder due to a recurring instance of that mythological Freudian strain, endemic to modernity, of 'unconscious' racism as a psychological pathology of mechanistic determinism, which can hence be rectified by police agents undergoing therapy as cultural sensitivity training. As such, the perpetual incarceration and accumulative slaughter of Black people by Empire is yet another tragic disclosure of structural-inert racist dehumanization inscribed in modernity, part-icularly during reconfigurations of western imper-ialist power as objective violence when confronted by an ascendant humanity challenging the sove-reign legitimacy of coloniality in the Raw.

Rupturing the coercive anonymity surrounding the neo-colonial police murder of Michael Brown, insurrection-in-itself, as a lived dynamic correlation between protest-as-resistance and spontaneous reb-ellion, reveals the constitutive role structural-inert violence inhabits within Empire, as the normative gaze sifts through claims of human subjectivity while persisting in severing the imperial main-stream of modernity from the socio-ontological underground. Thus, the murder of human 'being' finds diffusion through the 'law' itself, disciplining and punishing any assertion of Black subjectivity-as-human 'being' for unleashing socio-ontological potentialities of historical disequilibrium throughout the hegemonic contours of Empire "which does not confront us like a subject, facing us, but like an *environment*, that is hostile to us."[190]

The lived relation of coloniality in the Raw that positions western imperialist power against the assertion of Black subjectivity-as-human 'being' is irreconcilable, diminishes the socio-historical primacy of legal questions concerning innocence or guilt, suspends ethical norms, and unveils an exceptional antagonism that interrogates the very premise of sovereignty exercised by neo-colonial police. For by embodying the 'law', neo-colonial police agents wield a legitimate and legitimating violence, and are thus charged with the burden of continuously introducing and reconstituting the biopolitical alterity of modernity, in topographical coherence with a western imperialist continuum. Indeed, Empire, as the latest reconfiguration of a western imperialist continuum, is indicative of the lack of 'outside' positionality in relation to the globalized hegemony of structural-inert power. However, the contemporary consolidation of horizontal opposition within Empire only reinforces and highlights the potentialities of an ongoing vulnerability to vertical

---

[190] Tiqqun, *Introduction to Civil War*, p.171.

insurgency from below. "The Outside becomes the Inside, and the Inside now has no limits. What was formerly *present* in a certain defined place now becomes *possible everywhere*. What is turned inside out no longer exists in a positive way, in a concentrated form, but remains in a suspended state as far as the eye can see. It is the ultimate ruse of the system, the moment when it is most vulnerable and, at the same time, most impervious to attack."[191] Indeed, the lack of there being an 'outside' to Empire does nothing to negate the insurgent potentialities arising from its socio-ontological *under*ground.

Borders in the classical sense have been reduced to functional simulacra in the service of Empire, regulating movements of deterritorialized human populations and imposing coloniality on human 'being', while serving as an unchallenged political canopy under which a massive deregulation of the vulgar influence of capital continues unabated.

As geoterritorial delimitations erode, the margins of Empire can only be grasped as socio-ontological coordinates, topographically exposed by 'racial incidents' functioning as sudden sinkholes in the middle of heavy traffic, spontaneously interrupting the normative gaze and disclosing, at times by mere proximity to the glittering 'liberal-democratic' pres-

---

[191] Tiqqun, p.117.

tige of western imperialist metropoles, dark sobering glimpses into a vast underground of modernity peopled by *the wretched of the earth*. These biopolitical sinkholes, once having collapsed through the glossy surface of the imperial mainstream by way of 'racial incident', garner immediate attention and are judiciously 'fixed', rapidly patched up and appropriately restored, not by addressing racist dehumanization as the fundamental fault line of modernity, but rather, by the smooth application of yet another ideological layer of imperial concrete that hardens fast, under the guise of maintaining public order, 'racial' harmony and restoring the peace. And yet, relative peace for the imperial mainstream is subsidized by structural-inert racist oppression of human 'being' as objective violence against the socio-ontological underground.

Structural-inert violence preserves peace as statistical measures simulating progress through symbolic gains which are essentially provisional, divorced from historical impact, without any lasting meaning beyond the daily hyperproliferation of information and news as Spectacle. 'Protest-as-ritual event', carried out by good citizens of the imperial mainstream, legitimizes Spectacle by wholeheartedly embracing symbolic victory as an end in itself, thus miseducating the soul, in tandem with neo-colonial police violence against an ascendant humanity towards the biopolitical pacification of an exceptional antagonism arising from the assertion of Black subjectivity-as-human 'being'. "This peculiar kind of peace, this *armed* peace characteristic of imperial order, is felt to be all the more oppressive because it is itself the result of a total, mute, and continuous war. The stakes of the offensive are not to win a certain confrontation, but rather to make sure that the confrontation does not take place, to eliminate the event at the source, to prevent any surge of intensity"[192] from arising which might reintroduce *the wretched of the earth* to any constitutive socio-historical potentialities of emancipatory praxis against established global unjust power.

Internationally, this popular strategy of peacekeeping is often posited as humanitarian intervention, even as 'domestic' versus 'international' paradigms are now steadily disappearing as lost referentials of a bygone era, subsumed in Empire. This geohistorical erosion of sovereign distinction between 'domestic' and 'international' horizons of struggle, introduces a growing oppressive symmetry of biopolitical pacification embodied in neo-colonial 'law' enforcement. Thus, contemporary policing is clearly and explicitly predicated on paradigms of counterinsurgency as significantly reconstituted during western imperialist wars against

---

[192] Tiqqun, p.170.

internationalist decolonization struggles. "Imperial war has neither beginning nor end, it is a permanent process of pacification. The essential methodology and principles of Empire have been known for over fifty years. They were developed during the wars of decolonization during which the oppressive State apparatus underwent a decisive alteration."[193]

During such "a decisive alteration" of "the oppressive State apparatus", neo-colonial police Special Weapons and Tactics (S.W.A.T.) team formations were born in response to the growing insurgent threat of Black liberation praxis to western imperialist power during an era of intense geohistorical unrest spanning from the late 1960s until the mid 1970s. The S.W.A.T. team method of Law enforcement actually made its debut during a particular conflagration of these "wars of decolonization" between the Black Panther Party and the neo-colonial police force of Los Angeles in 1969 at 41st and Central.[194] Therefore, such explicit displays of

---

[193] Tiqqun, "Counterinsurgent Reconfigurations of Empire", *The Brotherwise Dispatch*, Vol.2, Issue#10, Dec/2013-Feb/2014. This is a revised English translation of what the French collective/journal Tiqqun published in 2001 as "and the State sank into the Imaginary Party" which relies heavily, though not exclusively on the excellent version found in Tiqqun, *This Is Not A Program*, pp.90-99.

[194] Matthew Fleischer, "Policing Revolution: How the LAPD's First Use of SWAT – a Massive. Military-Style Operation Against the Black Panthers – Was Almost its Last," *LA Times Magazine*,

overwhelming neo-colonial police force, as witnessed by the world during the early stages of the Ferguson Rebellion, that caused such disingenuous mainstream media uproar and social concern over police militarization, should not be regarded as a new and recent trend of excessive police intervention or rampant police militarization gone awry. Rather, the media generated Spectacle surrounding the response of established power to the Ferguson Rebellion displaced actual exposure of the Real of counterinsurgency as intrinsic to contemporary neo-colonial police procedure. "From then on the enemy was no longer an isolated entity, a foreign nation or a determined class, but somewhere lying in ambush amongst the population, without visible attributes. When necessary, the population *itself* became the enemy, the population as insurgent force."[195]

Yet another "decisive alteration" underway in New York City involves "the creation of a heavily armed unit to patrol areas of the city and respond to large-scale events, such as protests or terrorist attacks"[196] called the Strategic Response Group. The

---

April, 2011. For an excellent first-hand account check out Wayne Pharr, *Nine Lives of a Black Panther*, (Chicago: Lawrence Hill Books, 2014) pp.1-12.

[195] Tiqqun, p.91.

[196] nytimes.com, "N.Y.P.D. Plans Initiatives to Fight Terrorism and Improve Community Relations", J. David Goodman, JAN. 29, 2015. Emphasis mine.

normative gaze thus increases the imposition of social equivalence between "protests" and "terrorist attacks" as the Real. Even the stated ideological justification of making society "safe from crime, safe from terrorists, safe from disorder,"[197] does nothing to alleviate neo-colonial police violence from taking deadly aim at the assertion of Black subjectivity-as-human 'being' which is rendered by the normative gaze of structural-inert global power as an onto-logical reservoir of criminality, 'biopolitical danger', and socio-historical disequilibrium. Already, dynamic grassroots activist formations organizing around preventing the accumulative slaughter of Black people are experiencing the brunt of this particular reconfiguration of Empire as a "permanent process of pacification."

For amongst the "population *itself*", there exist rival anthropological currents of human subject-ivity. There is an imperial mainstream whose possibility of *becoming* "the enemy" is contingent upon both the pragmatic necessity of established power and the exercise of human agency in delib-erate opposition to structural-inert global injustice, as both Edward Snowden and Bradley/Chelsea Manning can bear ample witness. However, "population *itself*" is also comprised of a socio-

---

[197] gothamist.com, "A Visit With The 'Goon Squad': Meet The NYPD's Specially Trained Protest Police", Scott Heins, DEC. 17, 2015.

ontological underground for whom the probability of *becoming* the enemy is a distinct impossibility. Indeed, ever since the imposition of modernity upon the world by western imperialist power, our lot is actually that of already *being* the enemy by mere facticity of our existence, as indicative of that rational signification of subhumanity called 'race'. As such, 'race' becomes the materialistic anthropological vehicle of a lived experience of coloniality in the Raw, in which we find ourselves overdetermined-from-without by a western imperialist continuum imposing a biopolitical alterity, that *a priori* constitutes Black subjectivity, not even as an Other human 'being'-as-enemy, but rather as "the enemy" of human 'being' itself.[198]

What does it then mean when neo-colonial police officers brazenly leave Michael Brown's body exposed to the elements like a rotting animal carcass for several hours as an explicit reminder to Black community of the Real of unrelenting structural-inert violence implicating our temporality and 'being-in-the-world'? "At each moment at its existence, the police remind the State of the violence, the banality, and the darkness of its beginnings."[199] And yet, it is not only "the State" for whom historical memory awakens when faced with

---

[198] Jean-Paul Sartre, *Critique of Dialectical Reason Vol.1*, p.720.
[199] Tiqqun, *Introduction to Civil War*, p.105.

the existence of neo-colonial police, whose original institutional genesis is functionally located in the surveillance of Black community towards suppressing any assertion of Black subjectivity-as-human 'being', both before and after that era of direct formal human slavery endorsed by western imperialist power.[200] Indeed, after witnessing this flaunting of racist dehumanization in all its naked savagery, how significant are *any* changes in the sovereign relation between neo-colonial police and the lived orientation of Black community constituting new rhythms of protest-as-resistance and spontaneous rebellion against Empire?

Initially, the structural-inert violence of neo-colonial police succeeds in reaffirming the sovereignty of western imperialist power by a materialist reduction of human 'being' to 'objecthood' through the murder of Michael Brown, whose body remains sprawled out within a pool of his own blood in the middle of a street, during a sweltering hot day in Ferguson, Missouri.

And yet, at this point, let us not forget that the very socio-historical effectiveness and relentless ontological consistency of structural-inert violence against Black people exacted by neo-colonial police throughout Empire is definitively premised, first

---

[200] Sally E. Hadden, *Slave Patrols*, (Cambridge: Harvard University Press, 2003).

and foremost, upon the actual recognition of our ascendant humanity as its precautionary starting point. "This is the contradiction of racism, colonialism and all forms of tyranny: in order to *treat a man like a dog*, one must first recognize him as a man."[201] Thus the imposition of coloniality in the Raw upon human 'being' is absolutely predicated upon a comprehensive recognition of our irreducible agency and invulnerable potentialities towards constituting human subjectivity for its methodical effectiveness.

Indeed, for as more and more people bear witness to yet another example of such continuing atrocity against humanity, news rapidly spreads, people communicate, and begin to gather. Before long, crowds form and disperse, and form again. Michael Brown's body remains there on the street, mortally severed from human subjectivity by police bullets, unsettling a pervasive overdetermination-from-without that situates lived Black experience by inciting our radical imagination towards the Divine, as inconceivable social potentialities of justice beyond the Real of a western imperialist continuum. For as socio-historical impasse of tyranny confronts the Divine, the Real is no longer sufficient. For that which was once concretely evident and barely tolerated as 'that's just the way it is',

[201] Sartre, p.111.

now becomes an unbearable weight upon existence inspired by emancipatory potentialities of its socio-historical surpassing. An intersubjective resonance of Revolt begins to permeate Black community as diverse social formations of grassroots organizing struggle to keep pace with the gathering historical momentum towards protest-as-resistance and spontaneous rebellion against established global unjust power.

Insurrection-in-itself needs no justification, for it is a consequence of structural-inert oppression Returning to source. And yet, insurrection-in-itself does not occur in scientific adherence to iron laws of mechanistic causality set in motion by economic exploitation or racist dehumanization, but rather by the socio-ontological disposition of Black community as ascendant humanity in resistance against the structural-inert oppression inscribed in modernity as objective violence. The lived relevance of human 'being' as irreducible cipher of agency situated by a dialectic rhythm of intersubjective resonance towards one another and intermediations towards the world, encompasses all humanity.

For authentic recognition of situated consciousness, is not only contingent upon recognition of such 'presence-towards-self' in one another, but necessarily manifests itself against the Real through praxis, hence guaranteeing an inexhaustible reservoir of existential potentialities towards socio-historical liberation. This socio-ontological disposition is not only shared, but contributed to by any who, in choosing to fight back against the abdication of human subjectivity-as-lived universal, engage in emancipatory praxis against western imperialist power.

And yet, what is it about asserting the singularity of Black subjectivity-as-human 'being' through emancipatory praxis that unleashes an exceptional antagonistic reciprocity against Empire towards new potentialities of human subjectivity-as-lived universal? How is it that Black liberation praxis, regardless of whether framed as 'revolution', 'revolts against human slavery', 'maroonage', 'underground fugitive networks', 'abolitionism', 'civil war', 'civil rights struggle', 'Black power', 'ghetto rebellion', 'urban guerilla war', or 'decolonization', historically functions with unrivalled potency as a radical catalyst of ascendant humanity against western imperialist power? "In fact, the veiled slavery of the wage labourers in Europe needed the unqualified slavery of the New World as its pedestal."[202]

Insurrection-in-itself overcomes instrumentalist paradigms of beseeching established power for the attainment of objective political ends. As such, in

---

[202] Karl Marx, *Capital Vol.1*, (New York: Penguin Classics, 1867, 1990) p.925.

solidarity with our brothers and sisters during "the riots in the UK" and "the Paris banlieues in 2005", the postmodern lumpenproletariat have "no message to deliver" to the ruling power elite, for such a message would suggest the need for beginning a process of biopolitical pacification initiated by reasonable negotiations towards restoring 'peace' and 'order' within Empire rather than necessitating its Overturning as a fundamental structural transformation.[203] Lest we forget, this insurgent "challenge to the colonial world is not a rational confrontation of points of view. It is not a treatise on the universal, but the untidy affirmation of an original idea propounded as an absolute."[204] The universal cannot be quarantined within a treatise, it is decided in the streets of history. The diversity of its many discursive formulations, notwithstanding, such "an original idea" finds its contemporary enunciation as egalitarian geonational community *ad portas*.

Through the lived dynamic correlation of protest-as-resistance and spontaneous rebellion, an urgent ongoing communication ensues amongst *the wretched of the earth* situated throughout Empire: circu-

---

[203] Slavoj Zizek, "Shoplifters of the World Unite", *London Review of Books*, August 19, 2011.
http://www.lrb.co.uk/2011/08/19/slavoj-zizek/shoplifters-of-the-world-unite
[204] Frantz Fanon, *The Wretched of the Earth*, p.41.

lating between Los Angeles and Paris, between Tottenham and Ferguson, between Baltimore and Gaza, between New York City and Sao Paolo, between Chicago and Port-au-Prince. As such, choosing to draft "clear proposals"[205] with Molotov cocktails towards initiating small scale informal melees of exceptional antagonistic reciprocity between postmodern lumpenproletariat and neo-colonial police, forces the normative gaze of established power into an 'official' recognition of ascendant humanity through imperial declarations establishing an 'official state of emergency'. This 'official state of emergency' translates the 'unofficial' exceptional antagonism initiated by the assertion of Black subjectivity-as-human 'being' situated within modernity, from roaming socio-ontological coordinates of lived Black experience, into a comprehensive legal simulation of a territorially based suspension of 'law' as a 'state of exception' which thereby discloses the Real of our contemporary human situation.[206] "The tradition of the oppressed teaches us that the 'state of emergency' in which we live is not the exception but the rule. We must attain a

---

[205] Zizek, "Shoplifters of the World Unite".

[206] "*Being-outside, and yet belonging* – this is the topological structure of the state of exception." Giorgio Agamben, *State of Exception*, p.35.

consciousness of history that accords with this insight."[207]

Indeed, any epistemological "difficulty in conceiving of 'rioters' in Marxist terms as an instance of the emergence of the revolutionary subject"[208], aside from presupposing that any vulgar strain of Marxism can grasp insurrection-in-itself on its own terms without being sufficiently 'stretched' to account for coloniality in the Raw, actually serves as an important reminder of existing emancipatory tensions, between *oppositional* stances of rebellion originating within the imperial mainstream against advanced neo-liberal capitalist globalization, and *insurgent* orientations of Revolt originating from the socio-ontological underground of modernity against a western imperialist continuum. "Everything up to and including the very nature of pre-capitalist society, so well explained by Marx, must here be thought out again."[209]

Rebellion originating from within the imperial mainstream is *oppositional* by remaining existentially limited through its shared adherence to a materialist determinism and 'racist' anthropology as generated and ratified by a western imperialist continuum, even while opposing the dictates of

---

[207] Walter Benjamin, *Selected Writings Vol.4 1938-1940*, (Cambridge: Belknap/Harvard University Press, 2003) p.392.
[208] Zizek, "Shoplifters of the World Unite".
[209] Fanon, p.40.

global capital with a competing state communist or redemptive state socialist version of modernity. "They cannot let go of the *idee fixe* of the white working class 'saving' the world's humanity. Rooted in their preconceived notions, their undialectical ideas, is the deeply ingrained 'white nation ideal.' Socialism becomes, like capitalism, a white-nation conception, the great white working-class prerogative. The 'white man's burden' shifts from the capitalist's missionaries to the socialist's revolutionaries, whose duty to history is to lift the 'backward' peoples from their ignominious state to socialist civilization – even if the whites have to postpone this elevation abroad until they have managed to achieve it at home."[210]

Revolt originating from within the socio-ontological underground is *insurgent* by threatening an Overturning of the very paradigm of modernity itself, unencumbered from a blind fealty towards any restorative pretense of an era before the disaster of a western imperialist continuum. Such Revolt, thereby initiates lived potentialities for reconstituting human subjectivity-as-lived universal against the spiritual poverty of imperialist anthropology born out of concerted attempts towards a systematic violent grafting of human 'being' into 'objecthood' through *chattel* slavery which serves as historical

---

[210] Harold Cruse, *Rebellion or Revolution*, p.149.

precondition for the rise and triumph of global capital.[211]

As such, to suggest the supposed lack of any "visible attributes" in those whom Empire designates officially as "the enemy", is not only socio-historically false, and ideologically misleading, but indicative of a self-defeating, yet long standing, tradition of exercising an inappropriate amount of epistemological reliance on a western imperialist continuum with the supposed aim of resisting, undermining, and reforming western imperialist power. How else could Zizek, supposedly 'the most dangerous philosopher in the West', actually comment on the London Rebellion ignited after the murder of

---

[211] "Direct slavery is as much the pivot upon which our present day industrialism turns as are machinery, credit, etc. Without slavery there would be no cotton, without cotton there would be no modern industry. It is slavery which has given value to the colonies, it is the colonies which have created world trade, and world trade is the necessary condition for large-scale machine industry. Consequently, prior to the slave trade, the colonies sent very few products to the Old World, and did not noticeably change the face of the world. Slavery is therefore an economic category of paramount importance. Without slavery, North America, the most progressive nation, would be transformed into a patriarchal country. Only wipe North America off the map and you will get anarchy, the complete decay of trade and modern civilization. But to do away with slavery would be to wipe America off the map. Being an economic category, slavery has existed in all nations since the beginning of the world. All that modern nations have achieved is to disguise slavery at home and import it openly into the New World." Karl Marx, *The Poverty of Philosophy*, (Amherst: Prometheus Books, 1847, 1995) pp.121-2.

Mark Duggan by neo-colonial police violence, by stating that "on British streets during the unrest, what we saw was not men reduced to 'beasts', but the stripped-down form of the 'beast' produced by capitalist ideology."[212] This disparaging animalistic description of "what we saw", discloses a shared anthropological orientation between Zizek's allegedly radical discourse and the normative gaze of Empire in relation to the socio-ontological underground of modernity. Indeed, "at the deepest level of Western knowledge, Marxism introduced no real discontinuity".[213]

This epistemological reliance on a western imperialist continuum again resurfaces as Zizek attempts to reduce insurrection-in-itself to an oddly coded deracialized fiction sounding eerily derivative of racist reactionary clichés of 'Black on Black crime' that are indicative of a continuing discursive persistence of Social Darwinism. "The truth was that the conflict was between two poles of the underprivileged: those who have succeeded in functioning within the system versus those who are too frustrated to go on trying. The rioters' violence was almost exclusively directed against their own."[214] There is an uncanny theoretical dexterity involved in Zizek's reduction of protest-as-resistance and

---

[212] Zizek, "Shoplifters of the World Unite".

[213] Michel Foucault, *The Order of Things*, p.261.

[214] Zizek, "Shoplifters of the World Unite".

spontaneous rebellion to an "implicit admission of impotence"[215] by "rioters"[216] who in actuality communicated quite clearly that "their confrontations with the police made them feel 'powerful'"[217] while "others described how they threw stones and bottles, rammed police with wheelie bins and shouted 'F*ck the police.' Some spoke of how they targeted police property, setting fire to and vandalizing cars, vans and police stations, or deliberately trying to inflict injury on officers."[218] Even the Association of Chief Police Officers in Britain recognizes that "the disorder seen in August was unprecedented in its scale of violence and the way in which events escalated rapidly."[219] Indeed, why were 16,000 British police needed to quell such an "implicit admission of impotence"?

As such, regardless of whether it is because of, or in spite of, Zizek's philosophical leanings, neo-colonial police violence against human 'being' somehow becomes irrelevant in his critique, disappearing from the narrative entirely as the "two poles of the underprivileged" fighting amongst them-

---

[215] Ibid.
[216] Ibid.
[217] UK Riots 2011: Reading the Riots, "English riots were 'a sort of revenge' against the police", *The Guardian*, December 4, 2001. https://www.theguardian.com/uk/2011/dec/05/riots-revenge-against-police
[218] Ibid.
[219] Ibid.

selves reveals "the truth" of "the rioters violence" which is incredulously "not self-assertive".[220] Is this Lacanian *muthaf*cka* not Hegelian enough to recognize an unceasing dialectic confrontation between western imperialist power attempting to structurally sustain the recognition of its 'mastery' over an ascendant humanity that has chosen to resist? Maybe Kojeve can remind him that "the Master can never detach himself from the World in which he lives, and if this World perishes, he perishes with it. Only the Slave can transcend the given World (which is subjugated by the Master) and not perish. Only the Slave can transform the World that forms him and fixes him in slavery and create a World that he has formed in which he will be free. . . . Therefore, it is indeed the originally dependent, serving, and slavish Consciousness that in the end realizes and reveals the ideal of autonomous Self-Consciousness and is thus its 'truth'."[221] However, it is here that the Douglassian anti-slavery dialectic necessarily intervenes against the Hegelian Master-Slave dialectic and its interlocutors, for it is not through "the discipline of service and obedience" of slave labor that "the bondsman becomes conscious of what he truly is" and "acquires a mind of his

---

[220] Zizek, "Shoplifters of the World Unite".
[221] Alexandre Kojeve, *Introduction to the Reading of Hegel*, (Ithaca: Cornell University Press 1947, 1969) pp.29-30.

own".[222] Rather, it is through emancipatory praxis, "undignified as it was and as I fear was my narration of it", in confrontation against "the unjust cruel aggressions of a tyrant" that initiates a dialectic of Revolt which ruptures the paralysis of biopolitical alterity between Master and Slave by transcending mere role reversals of Mastery and Slavery towards bringing about 'the end of the world' that is constituted by, and subsumed in, the Raw coloniality of power between Master and Slave.[223]

Against Mignolo's sound critique[224] of his work, Zizek quickly reaches for Fanon, ably defending himself, and rightfully berating postcolonial eunuchs like Bhabha for watering down Fanon's insurgent philosophical orientation. And yet, when there is protest-as-resistance and spontaneous rebellion Returning to source in the streets of a western

---

[222] Hegel, *Phenomenology of Spirit*, (Oxford: Oxford University Press, 1977) p.118.

[223] Frederick Douglass, *Autobiographies*, p.591.

[224] In "Yes, We Can: Non-European Thinkers and Philosophers", aljazeera.com, 2-19-2013, Walter Mignolo revisits an argument he initiates in *The Darker Side of Western Modernity*, (Durham: Duke University Press, 2011) pp.243-250. Unfortunately, Mignolo ultimately disassociates the relevance of European philosophers from their relation to Empire, and retreats from universality, as if "dewesternization" and "polyversality" can be authentically carried to fruition by ignoring rather than confronting the normative gaze of a western imperialist continuum.

imperialist metropole, Fanon is suddenly out of reach as Zizek gleefully fondles the most ungainly aspects protruding from Arendt's lamentable discourse on violence and revolution.[225] Indeed, might the fact that Zizek's intellectual engagement consists in discursively dismissing and abandoning *the wretched of the earth* right at the lived crossroads between radical theory and emancipatory praxis, be the very source of his popularity within the imperial mainstream? No doubt, there is a clear difference between being 'the most dangerous philosopher *in* the West' and being the most dangerous philosopher *to* western imperialist power.

As such, f*ck you Zizek, and the ghost of Stalin you rode in on. For as outcasts "outside organized social space" originating from within both extremes of human subjectivity as those disenchanted with the imperial mainstream and those disenfranchised within the socio-ontological underground of modernity, postmodern lumpenproletariat definitively "fit much better the Hegelian notion of the 'rabble'" than anything close to resembling the self-serving imperial complicity befitting good citizens of Empire.[226] Indeed, there is no 'fixed' objective truth to be *found* in rioting, rather, it is through the lived truth

---

[225] Katherine Gines critique superbly takes Arendt to task on this very question. *Hannah Arendt and the Negro Question*, (Bloomington: Indiana University Press, 2014) pp.93-111.
[226] Zizek "Shoplifters of the World Unite".

of protest-as-resistance and spontaneous rebellion as insurrection-in-itself, that new emancipatory potentialities of meaning are *introduced* to the radical imagination.

Nationalist partisan politics with supposedly "clear agendas"[227] merely shadow dance in subservience to global capital with a 'played out' parliamentarian beat as poorly sampled from progressive Enlightenment mythology[228] which inspired previous generations towards culturally making imperial civil society more accessible to any who worship at the altar of Man-as-western bourgeois subjectivity. However, such sanguine 'liberal-democratic' posturing fundamentally ignores its continued symbiotic historical relation to the extreme and objective violence of coloniality as contemporary reconfigurations of western imperialist power continue to exact a tremendous lived expense from an ascendant humanity quarantined within the socio-ontological underground of modernity. The once potent 'wonderbread' cultural nationalist theology of social recognition, spiritual assimilation, civic participation and political representation, all coalescing under a biopolitical canopy of 'whiteness', no longer even suffices an imperial mainstream in severe anthropological panic faced with a totali-

---

[227] Ibid.
[228] Theodore Adorno and Max Horkheimer, *Dialectic of Enlightenment*.

tarian security culture eroding civil liberties coupled with impending shrouds of economic austerity imposed by the ruling power elite.

However, in spite of tremendous ideological bombardment and vast imperial assimilationist efforts to the contrary, the overwhelmingly colored face of incarcerated humanity necessitating the presservation of 'law and order' within a nation-state, still preposterously claiming to be the global standard bearer of 'liberal-democratic' utopian exceptionalism, explicitly discloses the 'racially' distinctive "visible attributes" that identify those of us who constitute the socio-ontological antithesis of maintaining a western imperialist continuum that is "safe from crime, safe from terrorists, safe from disorder".

The globalized sovereignty of Empire-as-western imperialist power is thus clearly predicated upon the anthropological severance of the mainstream from the underground, particularly through the rational signification of subhumanity referred to as 'race' that sustains a biopolitical alterity generated by an overdetermination-from-without subsumed in the Raw of coloniality that utilizes 'race' as an infallible source of "visible attributes" from thence to dispense with brutality and injustice on precisely such grounds. "This is to say violence against Black people is ontological and gratuitous as opposed to ideological and contingent."[229]   Indeed, violence is contingent amongst relations within the lived hemisphere of mainstream imperial subject-ivity.   However, violence takes on a more objective character positioned at the lived crossroads between imperial mainstream and socio-ontological under-ground of modernity.

And yet, among the enduring images of the Ferguson Rebellion is one of a group of brothers lighting Molotov cocktails intent on Returning stru-ctural-inert violence back to source against the occupying power of neo-colonial police force, while a woman whom under the normative gaze is easily identified as 'white', is seen assisting in the back-ground, engaged in emancipatory praxis with Black men distributing Molotov cocktails in confrontation against established unjust global power.   Should it matter that she may not be from the same neighbor-hood as those brothers?   And why do we assume that she is not?   Why exactly shouldn't she be there assisting a struggle for human liberation?   In what sense does her engagement in emancipatory praxis enunciate her understanding of human 'being'?   Is this a clear example of *outside* agitation?   What then does it mean when it is precisely her *outside* agita-

---

[229] Frank B. Wilderson III, "Gramsci's Black Marx: Whither the Slave in Civil Society?", *Social Identities*, Vol.9, #2, 2003. See also *The Brotherwise Dispatch*, Vol.2, Issue#1, Dec/2009-Feb/2010.

tion that situates her 'being-in-the-world' *inside* the trajectory of an ascendant humanity? Wherever humanity is oppressed, you will find those who refuse to sit back idly and rest on the anthropological guarantee of 'white' identity and imperial mainstream privilege as a tacit biopolitical coalition between ruling power elite and toiling proletariat masses against the socio-ontological underground of modernity. However, the question has never been whether or not 'whites' can overcome their 'whiteness' towards a shared humanity through engagement in emancipatory praxis, but rather, just how long they intend to sustain such egalitarian nobility by remaining locked, arm in arm, with arms, in the struggle for human liberation once rounds of counterinsurgent blowback from global structural-inert power begin to focus in their direction?

Since its inception, the working class has continuously confronted the choice of whether to remain well behaved dutiful citizens subsisting on the economic leftovers of imperial hegemony, belligerent activists wanting to enjoy more and more of a just share of the economic spoils of Empire, or uniting in affirmation of human 'being' with *the wretched of the earth* on a trajectory of geonational insurrection-for-itself against a western imperialist continuum. Its glory days as a globally 'racialized' buffer class are nearing an ignominious end.[230]

As such, Empire's concern over "the population as insurgent force" is urgently distinct from concern over the population as 'oppositional force'. Empire threatens opposition with assimilation, while simultaneously threatening insurgency with decimation, for should mainstream opposition and underground insurgency begin uniting through emancipatory praxis against western imperialist power, symbolic cultural progress cedes ground to lived socio-historical movement towards egalitarian geonational community. Indeed, J. Edgar Hoover's declaration that "the Black Panther Party, without question, represents the greatest threat to the internal security of the country"[231] is no hyperbole. For by engaging

---

[230] "Therefore, any conception of "socialist revolution" simply in terms of the working people of the United States, failing to recognize the full scope of interests of the most oppressed peoples of the world, is a conception of a fight for a particular privileged interest, and is a very dangerous ideology. While the control and use of the wealth of the Empire for the people of the whole world is also in the interests of the vast majority of the people in this country, if the goal is not clear from the start we will further the preservation of class society, oppression, war, genocide, and the complete emiseration of everyone, including the people of the US." Karin Asbley, Bill Ayers, Bernardine Dohrn, John Jacobs, Jeff Jones, Gerry Long, Home Machtinger, Jim Mellen, Terry Robbins, Mark Rudd, Steve Tappis, "Weatherman Manifesto", *New Left Notes*, June 18, 1969.

[231] United Press International (UPI) in "FBI Director Blacks Black Panthers," *Oakland Tribune*, July 15, 1969, 17. Much respect to Joshua Bloom and Waldo E. Martin, Jr. and their outstanding

in an exceptional antagonistic reciprocity fueled by the assertion of Black subjectivity-as-human 'being' against western imperialist power, the Black Panther Party and the Black Liberation Army were never an *oppositional* threat intent on taking over the nation-state apparatus, rather, as a protean cipher of emancipatory praxis facilitating a lived unity-as-diversity between postmodern lumpenproletariat elements within the imperial mainstream and the socio-ontological underground, they constituted an *insurgent* threat towards introducing geohistorical disequilibrium against the sovereign legitimacy of the nation-state paradigm itself.

Indeed, how is it that Assata Shakur peacefully living in Cuba as an exile still threatens established global unjust power? What then does recapturing Assata Shakur really mean to the normative gaze of a western imperialist continuum?[232] And how is one supposed to interpret renewed attempts in 2007 to round up, arrest and retry former Black Panther Party and Black Liberation Army members based on false accusations and charges which didn't even

---

work *Black Against Empire* (Berkeley: University of California Press, 2013) for unearthing the actual source article.

[232] In 2013 Shakur's bounty was raised to 2 million dollars and her name is still included in both domestic and international lists of 'terrorists'. Nick Chiles, "FBI Puts 2 Million Bounty on Assata Shakur, Calls Her Most Wanted Terrorist", atlantablackstar.com. For her story, check out - Assata Shakur, *Assata: An Autobiography*, (Chicago: Lawrence Hill Books, 1987).

hold up back in 1971?[233] No doubt, the sovereign prestige of Empire is invaluable, for "prestige bars any serious attack on power. . . . in the process of things, the prestige of power emerges roughly in that period when power does not have to exercise its underlying basis – violence."[234] What Jackson surprisingly overlooks however, is how the normative gaze veils the assertion of Black subjectivity-as-human 'being' with a coercive anonymity, thus allowing for a continuous renewal of structural-inert violence against humanity while simultaneously enjoying a sovereign prestige associated with maintaining the peace.

It is precisely this sovereign prestige-as-imperial peace that is perpetually called into question by the assertion of Black subjectivity-as-human 'being' that constitutes an exceptional antagonism disclosing an anthropological "threshold of indeterminacy between democracy and absolutism"[235] which is imposed as biopolitical pacification upon a deterritorialized population through miseducation, surveillance, incarceration, torture, and accumulative slaughter.

---

[233] Jaxon Van Derbeken and Marisa Lagos, "Ex-Militants Charged in S.F. Police Officer's '71 Slaying at Station", SFGATE.com, 1-23-2007.
http://www.sfgate.com/bayarea/article/Ex-militants-charged-in-S-F-police-officer-s-71-2654930.php
[234] George Jackson, *Blood in My Eye*, (Baltimore: Black Classics Press, 1971) p.50.
[235] Giorgio Agamben, *State of Exception*, p.3.

"Every fiction of a nexus between violence and Law disappears here: there is nothing but a zone of anomie, in which a violence without any juridical form acts."[236]

Therefore, what are we really *seeing* during the Ferguson Rebellion? What does it mean when a Black woman faces heavily militarized neo-colonial police agents drawing guns and aiming at her very humanity, with an unrepentantly emancipatory gaze and a welcoming gesture of resistance by raising her hands above her head while enunciating with forceful clarity: 'Hands Up Don't Shoot'? Is she not daringly beckoning these sentinels of Empire away from the shelter of sovereign prestige towards that *precipice of anomie* where an exceptional antagonistic reciprocity might resume as emancipatory praxis against western imperialist power?

Through her gestures and enunciations Black community recognizes our own all too human agency, and through our emancipatory reawakening, ascendant humanity recognizes itself. Indeed, who dares lay claim to a historical narrative of human freedom, and yet still sit unmoved by the tragic execution of Darren Seals, a fundamental presence in the Ferguson Rebellion, found shot in the head inside a burning car, a week after neo-

---

[236] Agamben, p.59.

colonial police agents pulled guns on him and his fourteen-year-old brother with an overt warning to "pick your enemies better"?[237]

Protest-as-resistance questions the very premise of how violence without legalized form still persists with legal sanction, while spontaneous rebellion besieges the precipice of anomie through the Return of structural-inert violence back to source. Insurrection-in-itself thus introduces the conditions of possibility for a radical seizure of lived experience within the precipice of anomie, from an imperial hegemony embodied in neo-colonial police agents through whom 'law' is preserved by sovereign force that displaces the social function of 'rights' and historical relevance of 'legality', imposing relations of power that renew the topographical coherence and reconstitute the pure originary violence of coloniality in the Raw. "The point is that the police – contrary to public opinion – are not merely an administrative function of law enforcement; rather, the police are perhaps the place where the proximity and the almost constitutive exchange between violence and right that characterizes the figure of the sovereign is shown more nakedly than anywhere else."[238]   As such, resisting neo-colonial

---

[237] shout out to The Advise Show TV -
https://www.youtube.com/watch?v=j6Td4GXhaac
[238] Agamben, *Means Without End*, (Minneapolis: University of Minnesota Press, 2000) p.103.

police violence interrogates the socio-ontological reach and sovereign legitimacy of a western imperialist continuum.

Structural-inert violence anchors the sovereign legitimacy of Empire to lived Black experience, gratuitously introducing modalities of 'social death'[239] in its wake which can only be overcome through emancipatory praxis. Indeed, authentic emancipatory praxis, because of the structural-inert relation between lived Black experience and modernity, does not cease with the prospect of freeing Black community from Empire in geohistorical exclusivity, although that is where we must necessarily begin; for Black liberation inherently contains within its emancipatory trajectory a socio-ontological imperative for the universal liberation of humanity itself. The burden of lived Black experience as human 'being' transcending an originary imposition of human enslavement by western imperialist power that structures the contemporary ordering of the world as modernity, necessarily consists in radical socio-ontological potentialities towards seizing responsibility for ensuring a universal trajectory of human liberation. Such is L'Ouverture's lament: What further tragedy awaits us, spread throughout the Black Diaspora, we who must shoulder the

---

[239] Orlando Patterson, *Slavery and Social Death*, (Cambridge: Harvard University Press, 1982).

burden of asserting Black subjectivity-as-human 'being' and its geohistorical emancipatory implications against Empire? Indeed, lived Black experience is a singular phenomenon without geohistorical precedent, and this is definitively why its socio-ontological relevance is universal.

The lived inertia to spiritually assimilate into an advanced neo-liberal capitalist hegemony has never been greater. And yet, it is precisely the Return of geohistorical momentum as manifest in the Ferguson Rebellion that intersubjectively resonates amongst *the wretched of the earth* with unprecedented socio-ontological gravity, inciting the radical imagination towards new potentialities of emancipatory praxis against Empire that show no signs of abating. For the prestige of Empire erodes in confrontation against emancipatory praxis which transforms an exceptional antagonism into an exceptional antagonistic reciprocity, thus disclosing structural-inert violence masquerading as peacekeeping which is the very condition of its sovereign legitimacy.

Insurrection-in-itself enunciates a radical Yearning for discontinuity within a western imperialist continuum arising from the socio-ontological underground as emancipatory potentialities of human 'being' which are irredeemable within modernity as imposed by western imperialist power, thus necessitating a fundamental anthropological reorientation at the root of any geohistorical movement towards social justice. Insurrection-in-itself thus Returns to established unjust global power as an emancipatory correspondence of ascendant humanity disclosing waves of geohistorical transition repeatedly crashing against a western imperialist continuum, for even now, the shores of Empire are flooding with adversity . . .

Black Rage as lucidity – Against a biological determinism that clinically translates existential respon-
ses of human 'being' confronting the objective
violence and unaccountable oppression of Empire
into a spiritually pacifying epistemology of neurological disorders and psychological pathologies,
lived manifestations of Black Rage threaten to overwhelm the normative gaze with an unheralded discursive lucidity of socio-ontological Revolt. Indeed,
far from irrational, Black Rage summons the primacy of human 'being' as irreducible agency towards
overcoming the encroaching reflexive attrition of
the normative gaze upon our kinetic distance of
interiority. "When his rage erupts, he rediscovers
his unmoored accountability and comes to know his
being insofar as he constitutes his subjectivity."[240]

As day turns to nightfall in Ferguson, Missouri,
news spreads around the world of yet another
grand jury, refusing to indict yet another neo-
colonial police officer for the murder of yet another
Black man. This time it's a Ferguson grand jury
refusing to issue an indictment against the police
agent who murdered Michael Brown, finding no
rational grounds or legal basis from which to proceed with criminal charges that might temporarily
disturb the sovereign legitimacy of neo-colonial

---

[240] Jean-Paul Sartre, Preface to Frantz Fanon's *The Wretched of
the Earth*, p.21. Modified translation my own.

police violence against human 'being'. A large indignant crowd of ascendant humanity gathers directly in front of the Ferguson Police Department. Michael Brown's mother begins to speak about such a profound tragedy, and is soon engulfed in sorrow.

"Everybody want me to be calm, do you know how dem bullets hit my son?"[241]

Now crying profusely, her husband makes his way up onto the platform and consoles her amidst proclamations of support from the crowd that ultimately evolve into enunciations like *"f*ck the police"* and *"we gon' get justice"*, brimming with inter-subjective resonance of even more waves of protest-as-resistance against neo-colonial police as the "instituted go-betweens, the spokesmen"[242] who translate the sovereign legitimacy of western imperialist power in the unambiguous language of violence to Black community. Michael Brown's stepfather then turns around in sheer and utter defiance of Empire and speaks.

*"Burn this muthaf*cka down, burn this b*tch down!"*

Black Rage as a piercing clarity of affective indignance of consciousness venturing towards voicing the incommunicable, discloses "an utterly naked declivity where an authentic upheaval can be

---

[241] Transcription based on
https://www.youtube.com/watch?v=_39_MSAjmp0
[242] Fanon, *The Wretched of the Earth*, p.38.

born",[243] thus spiritually galvanizing the exceptional antagonism of lived Black experience as a socio-ontological phenomenon without geohistorical precedent.[244] And yet, is not this exceptional antagonism that very measure by which the universality of the human condition interrogates the Real?

---

[243] Fanon, *Black Skin, White Masks*, p.8.

[244] Frank B. Wilderson III, "Gramsci's Black Marx: Whither the Slave in Civil Society?", *Social Identities*, Vol.9, #2, 2003, begins with an epigraph of historian Eugene Genovese from *Boston Review* Oct/Nov 1993, sharing in this understanding that "The Black experience in this country has been a phenomenon without analog." See also *The Brotherwise Dispatch*, Vol.2, Issue#1, Dec/2009-Feb/2010.

lumpenproletariat vendetta as tragic Return – A mother is murdered in front of her son.[245] A hard-working father is assassinated in front of his wife and child.[246] A leading young activist associated with the Ferguson Rebellion is executed by a bullet to the head before being lit on fire and left to burn inside a car.[247] A Father is murdered while reading and wielding a book inside a parked car as he waits to pick up his son from elementary school.[248] The sovereign legitimacy and impunity with which neo-colonial police inscribe, enable and renew struct-ural-inert violence against the assertion of Black subjectivity-as-human 'being' only begins to attest to compelling emancipatory human imperatives towards the Return of such objective violence back to genesis as a phenomenon of diverse modalities and astounding consistency.

Still, the normative gaze permeates the imperial mainstream with shuddering social incredulity, ont-ological shock and historical disbelief, whenever

[245] "Korryn Gaines, Cradling Child and Shotgun, is Fatally Shot by Police", Wesley Lowery, washingtonpost.com, August 2nd 2016.
[246] "Minnestoa Gov Calls Traffic Stop Shooting Absolutely Appalling at All Levels'", Camila Domonoske, Bill Chappell, NPR.org, July 7th, 2016.
[247] "Ferguson Protest Leader Darren Seals Shot and Found Dead in a Burning Car", Lois Beckett, theguardian.com, September 7th, 2016.
[248] "Keith Lamont Scott, 5 Fast Facts You Need to Know", heavy.com, September 20th, 2016.

postmodern lumpenproletariat decide to engage in armed vendettas against Empire. Throughout the Black Diaspora however, the Return is often met with competing expressions of vehement disapproval and iconoclastic sanction. Indeed, voices of irreverent endorsement exist side by side exhorttations of outright condemnation. And yet, is anyone amongst us really startled, or even remotely struck by sentiments within the affective vicinity of astonishment? For to express surprise at the Return of racist dehumanizing violence back to source requires an uncommon degree of Bad Faith[249] in relation to the Raw coloniality of lived Black experience within a western imperialist continuum.[250]

Lumpenproletariat vendetta does not merely originate from the intersubjective resonance between specific neo-colonial police agents who commit

---

[249] Lewis R. Gordon, *Bad Faith and Anti-Black Racism*.

[250] "In the same way the people make use of certain episodes in the life of the community in order to hold themselves ready and to keep alive their revolutionary zeal. For example, the gangster who holds up the police set on to track him down for days on end, or who dies in single combat after having killed four or five policemen, or who commits suicide in order not to give away his accomplices – these types light the way for the people, form the blueprints for action and become heroes. Obviously, it's a waste of breath to say that such-and-such a hero is a thief, a scoundrel, or a reprobate. If the act for which he is prosecuted by the colonial authorities is an act exclusively directed against a colonialist person or colonialist property, the demarcation line is definite and manifest. The process of identification is automatic." Fanon, *The Wretched of the Earth*, p.69.

singularly heinous injustices against humanity and the particular recipients of such objective violence themselves. Rather, the decision to embark upon such a vendetta, as neo-colonial police murder of human 'being' continues accelerating the accumulative slaughter of Black community-as-ascendant humanity, is indicative of a heightening sensitivity amongst postmodern lumpenproletariat as displaced spiritual outsiders experiencing the human condition through an intersubjective resonance of lived solidarity with brothers and sisters being unscrupulously murdered by a blatant and uninhibited tyranny. This intersubjective resonance bears witness to the constitutive rhythm of human 'being' in movement as praxis towards *human subjectivity-as-lived universal* existing through an intermediary gaze that recognizes shared potentialities for 'being-in-the-world'. "From the moment that you and your people are slaughtered as dogs, you have no other recourse but to use all and every means at your command, to reconstitute the primacy of your human subjectivity. You must therefore bring as much heavy pressure as you can to bear upon the body of your torturer, in order that his soul, which is lost somewhere, may finally find its way back the universal significance of humanity."[251]

---

[251] Fanon, p.295. Modified translation mine own.

Ismaaiyl Brinsley scopes out the scene while walking right past two neo-colonial police agents who are sitting inside a patrol car preparing for counterinsurgency drills near Myrtle and Tompkins Avenues in Brooklyn, New York City. After crossing the street, Brinsley purposefully doubles back, ambushing them, firing four shots from his 9 millimeter handgun at close range through the passenger's side window, tragically cutting short the lives of two neo-colonial police officers. Not long afterwards, Ismaaiyl Brinsley takes his own life with the same pistol at a subway station nearby, thereby disdainfully retreating into the shelter of his own mortality from an overwhelming vertigo[252] of praxis which allows him to breach the precipice of anomie with the following intentionality: "I'm Puttin Wings On Pigs Today. They Take 1 Of Ours...... Let's Take 2 of Theirs #ShootThePolice #RIPErivGardner #RIPMikeBrown This May Be My Final Post... I'm Putting Pigs In A Blanket". And yet, the normative gaze of established power dismisses the clear intentionality of Brinsley's enunciation,[253] thus structurally negating any recognition

---

[252] "Vertigo is anguish to the extent that I am afraid not of falling over the precipice, but of throwing myself over." Sartre, *Being and Nothingness*, p.65-66.

[253] "Ismaaiyl Brinsley: 5 Fast Facts You Need to Know", heavy.com, December 20th, 2014. "Police Union Links Cop Killings to Protests; NYPD Critics Condemn Shootings", Darran Simon, Ted Phillips, newsday.com, December 21st, 2014.

of his human agency and further obfuscating the tragic correlation between postmodern lumpenproletariat vendetta as a consequential Return of globalized structural-inert violence and the assertion of Black subjectivity-as-human 'being'. [254]

Initial police reports in Dallas, Texas of two snipers at elevated positions firing upon neo-colonial police agents from undisclosed triangulated coordinates at the close of an evening of peaceful civic protests against the political, institutional and legal unaccountability of police for the accumulative slaughter of human 'being', eventually evolves into a narrative of Micah Xavier Johnson tragically killing five neo-colonial police and wounding another seven officers of the imperialist occupying force "during a wild series of gun battles that stretched for blocks."[255] As crossfire begins subsiding, Johnson, "wielding an assault rifle and a handgun, held the police off for hours in a parking garage."[256] Though vastly outnumbering Johnson, neo-colonial police are ultimately unable to convince him to surrender, or overtake him by sheer force of arms, they soon come to grips with the almost certain prospect of even more police casualties should the armed stru-

---

[254] Lewis R. Gordon, *Fanon and the Crisis of European Man*, pp.68-83.
[255] "How the Dallas Shooting Unfolded", Yousur Al-Hlou, John Woo, nytimes.com, July 8, 2016.
[256] Ibid.

ggle continue. As Johnson's concerted Yearning to resist and sheer willingness to wager his own life tellingly breaks down the collective determination of neo-colonial police agents to risk their own lives any further, a C-4 explosive "delivered by a remote-controlled robot"[257] not only compensates for their spiritual reluctance, but actually succeeds in killing Johnson, thus ending an impasse of Douglassian dialectic resistance. Afterwards, the normative gaze of western imperialist power enunciates itself through its most obviously recognizable mouthpiece: "We will learn more, undoubtedly, about their twisted motivations, but let's be clear: There are no possible justifications for these attacks or any violence towards law enforcement".[258]

Early Sunday morning in Baton Rouge, Louisiana, neo-colonial police respond to a 911 call by a woman describing a man carrying an assault rifle walking around an area in close proximity to a gas station near Airline Highway. Arriving officers soon locate that man behind a cosmetics supply store; within seconds Gavin Eugene Long tragically guns down three neo-colonial police agents while wounding another three before a long-range sniper shot sends him to his own tragic death. Antici-

---

[257] Ibid.
[258] President Barack Obama quoted in "Chaos After the Gunshots in Dallas", Yara Bishara, Malachy Browne, nytimes.com, July 8, 2016.

pating the normative gaze of Empire encroaching upon the lived rhythm of his praxis and draining any emancipatory implications from his armed vendetta, Long left plenty of conversational elaborations accessible to the multitude, as a discursive counterweight towards preserving his intentionality while preparing to breach the precipice of anomie.

"Oh, and this is very important, I wanted to let y'all know. Cause if anything happen with me, cause I'm an alpha male, I stand up, I stand firm and I stand for mine. Til the end, til the last day on this, in this flesh, but I am not the flesh, I am not the body, I have a body. But I just wanna let y'all know. Don't affiliate me with nothin'. . . . No, I'm affiliated with the spirit of justice, nothin' else, nothin' more, nothin' less. . . . I thought my own thoughts, I made my own decisions, I'm the one who gotta listen to the judgement. That's it, and my heart is pure."[259]

Structural-inert violence against the assertion of Black subjectivity-as-human 'being' inscribes modernity itself, therefore rendering it objective and unaccountable. And yet the very gratuitousness and unaccountability of such oppressive violence tempts the Return with tragic indiscriminacy against Empire. Postmodern lumpenproletariat vendetta, as a constitutive project of situated consciousness

---

[259] Transcription based on https://www.youtube.com/watch?v=XAsJe129sRg, Shout out to *Hezakya News*.

succumbing to such temptation of resentment, temporarily and disruptively reorients the gravitational pull of unaccountable violence within the precipice of anomie away from the socio-ontological underground and towards western imperialist power; though ultimately unable to sustain itself as a lived trajectory towards emancipatory praxis.[260] As such, lumpenproletariat vendetta appropriates the fugitive sovereignty of *outlaw* subjectivity towards interrogating that force of 'law' which itself exists *outside* formal legality in direct correlation to continual reconfigurations of the sovereign legitimacy of Empire against an exceptional antagonism introduced by the assertion of Black subjectivity-as-human 'being'.

A funeral in Queens, New York meant to honor the first of two officers who were vengefully assassinated by Ismaaiyl Brinsley as payback for the neo-colonial police murders of Eric Garner and Michael Brown, becomes an unmitigated Spectacle of western imperialist power. "For the funeral was as much about policing and those who attack it as about a single man. Besides the usual official presence of the governor, the mayor and the police commissioner, this ceremony brought the vice president of the United States."[261] This Spectacle, as ideological materialization of the normative gaze,

---

[260] Fanon, p.139.
[261] "A Sea of Blue, Mourning the First of Two Slain Comrades", N. R. Kleinfield, nytimes.com, December 26, 2014.

aids in suppressing potentialities for social recognition of ventures towards historical agency, and hence loosens our already tentative grasp on realizing their full emancipatory significance. Is the funeral being utilized as an attempt to stop the floodgates of protest-as-resistance and spontaneous rebellion which have been further unloosed since the aftermath of Hurricane Katrina, and ultimately coming to the fore in Tottenham, Ferguson, Baltimore, Chicago, and Charlotte? Will it succeed in postponing the Return until the passing of another hour, another day, another year, or another decade? "The turnout was extraordinary. Though no reliable count was made, it appeared that more than 20,000 police officers came to Queens, from as far away as Wisconsin and California and England, some driving through the night to make it. Bordering streets were shut to traffic for blocks around. Traffic lights continued to change their colors, but there was no traffic, nothing but thick rows of police officers as far as anyone could see."[262] What is it about the relation between postmodern lumpenproletariat vendetta and the permanent immanence of neo-colonial police violence brought to bear upon lived Black experience that provokes such a Spectacular response? Could it be that the *precipice of anomie* is as much a dislocative historical vulnerab-

---

[262] Ibid.

ility of western imperialist power as biopolitical conduit of tyranny?

Douglass discursively initiates an insurgent philosophical interrogation of this exact question in "Is It Right and Wise To Kill a Kidnapper?"[263] And yet, the question now before us is not whether it is right and wise to eulogize a copkiller. Rather, within the tragic geohistorical context of modernity as imposed by western imperialist power and inscribed with the Raw coloniality of originary dehumanizing violence, would not such a eulogy be always already untimely? Indeed, for with regards to Brinsley, Johnson and Long, or anyone else choosing to confront the occupying neo-colonial police force that embodies the sovereign legitimacy of tyranny and oppression by Returning structural-inert violence back to genesis; does not history always already guarantee their ultimate, though albeit untimely, absolution?

---

[263] Frederick Douglass, "Is It Right and Wise to Kill a Kidnapper?", *Frederick Douglass' Paper*, June 2, 1854, included in *The Life and Writings of Frederick Douglass, Vol.2, Pre-Civil War Decade*, edited by Philip S. Foner, (New York: International Publishers, 1975) pp.284-289.

imperial equilibrium as disaster – As the globalized administrative personality of Empire gradually unhinges, while repeatedly shifting horizontally between structural-inert poles of neocolonial and colonial orientations, temptations to foreclose insurgent philosophical discourse into oppositional frameworks of partisan political maneuvering within each respective nationally appropriate paradigm of the imperial mainstream gather momentum. This horizontal Spectacle of oppositional rhetoric and electoral gamesmanship between neo-liberal, neo-conservative, and neo-fascist orientations, aims toward ideologically undermining imperatives of Revolt which challenge and confront western imperialist power from a position of vertical insurgency arising out of the socio-ontological under-ground of modernity.

The disaster that engulfs *the wretched of the earth* consists in a merciless geohistorical continuity of western imperialist power which submerges and drowns the ascendant humanity of Black community in objective violence and miseducation of soul. As such, ongoing crises in the administration of capital and preservation of hegemony within the imperial mainstream are openings towards potentialities of emancipatory praxis. Indeed, the question that haunts the radical imagination is not whether the cost of 'protest-as-resistance' and spontaneous rebellion is becoming too steep, but rather, whether the ongoing price of 'protest-as-ritual event' has taken too much of an existential toll on lived potentialities of human agency towards insurrection-for-itself?

For even when contemporary neo-fascist elements undertake 'democratic' seizures of the nation-state apparatus, does this not unveil the naked face of Empire without its accompanying sovereign prestige? And yet, has it not been under this very sovereign prestige that the inherent poverty of oppositional thought also finds comfort and shelter? Indeed, regardless of which faction of the ruling power elite wields the administrative apparatus of the nation-state, Black community-as-ascendant humanity remains exposed to coloniality in the Raw as an unremitting violence of socio-historical oppression that is regulated and maintained by the civic stability of imperial society.

And yet, what exactly should be understood by mainstream fluctuations in the outward geopolitical personality of Empire throughout the standard bearing metropoles of imperial civil society? As totalitarian security culture and the contemporary international crisis of immigrants and refugees coalesce and disclose an approaching horizon of geonational imperatives, are there signs that a more structurally fundamental transition is taking place in the globalized relations between a western imperialist continuum and *the wretched of the earth*?

geonational imagination ad portas – Geonational insurrection is at the gates: the decisive horizon of fundamental socio-historical change is shifting, thus exerting a revitalizing epistemological pressure upon the radical imagination. As such, the workings of a geonational imagination involve recognizing the borderless imperatives of egalitarian community encompassing a worldwide trajectory towards emancipatory praxis summoning lived potentialities of human unity-as-diversity as an authentic *zeitgeist* of social justice unconstrained by the normative gaze of Empire. Contemporary reconfigurations of Empire[264] sustain the sovereign legitimacy of western imperialist power through advanced neo-liberal capitalist globalization that deregulates capital in correspondence with the hyperregulation of *the wretched of the earth*, even as the imperial

---

[264] Kwame Nkrumah, *Neo-Colonialism: The Last Stage of Imperialism*, (London: Panaf Books, 1965, 1970). *Return to the Source: Selected Speeches of Amilcar Cabral*, Edited by Africa Information Service, (New York: Monthly Review Press, 1973). Benedict Anderson, *Imagined Communities*, (London: Verso, 1991). Michael Hardt and Antonio Negri, *Empire*, (Cambridge: Harvard University Press, 2000). Antonio Negri, *Empire and Beyond*. Tiqqun, *Introduction to Civil War*. Tiqqun, *This is Not a Program*. Nikhil Pak Singh, *Black is a Country*, (Cambridge: Harvard University Press, 2004). Walter Mignolo, *Local Histories/Global Designs*, (Princeton: Princeton University Press, 2000). Walter Mignolo, *The Darker Side of Western Modernity*. *Coloniality At Large*, Edited by Mabel Morana, Enrique Dussel, and Carlos A. Jauregui. Immanuel Wallerstein, *The Essential Wallerstein*, (New York: The New Press, 2000).

mainstream is held hostage through a totalitarian security culture that ideologically preserves the nation-state as ultimate horizon and fundamental guarantor of geohistorical relevance.

Nationalism is dead. Cleaver and Newton's insurgent theoretical interventions while they were still united in the Black Panther Party make this abundantly clear. "We called ourselves Black nationalists because we thought that nationhood was the answer. Shortly after that we decided that what we really needed was revolutionary nationalism, that is, nationalism plus socialism. After analyzing conditions a little more, we found that it was impractical and even contradictory. Therefore we went to a higher level of consciousness. We saw that in order to be free we had to crush the ruling circle and therefore we had to unite with the peoples of the world. So we called ourselves Internationalists. We sought solidarity with the peoples of the world. We sought solidarity with what we thought were the nations of the world. But then what happened? We found that because everything is in a constant state of transformation, because of the development of technology, because of the development of mass media, because of the firepower of the imperialist, and because of the fact that the United States is no longer a nation but an empire, nations could not exist, for they did not

have the criteria for nationhood. Their self-determination, economic determination, and cultural determination has been transformed by the imperialists
and the ruling circle. They were no longer nations .
. . *because nations have been transformed into
communities of the world.*"[265]

Advanced neo-liberal capitalist globalization continues consolidating state socialist and state communist variants of western imperialist power under
the aegis of Empire, respecting no paradigm suggesting ultimate geohistorical reconciliation within
the contours of the nation-state.[266]   And yet those
who claim to raise the banners of opposition to
Empire still find themselves immersed in an

---

[265] Huey P. Newton, *To Die For the People*, (San Francisco: City
Lights Books, 1972, 2009) pp.30-2. Emphasis in the original.
[266] "Various countries, which we thought were our friends and
allies to the end, are now making a separate peace with our sworn
enemy, the fascist imperialist U.S. government and ruling class.
The coming into view of the dialogue and negotiations between
the United States government and the government of the Peoples
Republic of China should be the final signal necessary for each
and every one of us to sit up and take notice. . . . They are quickly
resolving contradictions between capitalism and socialism,
between Christians and Jews, between Catholics and Protestants.
Their continued support for the racist colonialism of Portugal in
Africa, their stepped up aid and support of South Africa and
Southern Rhodesia, and added to this is our own experience,
bloody and brutal, which clearly indicates that the long-range plan
of the fascists for Afro-Americans has nothing to do with any
peace, harmony and brotherhood." Eldridge Cleaver, "Towards a
People's Army", *Target Zero*, (New York: Palgrave Macmillan,
1971, 2006) p.222.

epistemological density of ideological bondage to nationalist eschatology. Archaic reactionary fealty to the vested interests of the nation veers closer and closer towards socio-historical irrelevance when faced with the racist dehumanization and hyper-exploitative demands of western imperialist power. "For the nation-state cannot exist once its principle of equality before the law has broken down. Without this legal equality, which originally was destined to replace the older laws and orders of the feudal society, the nation dissolves into an anarchic mass of over– and underprivileged individuals. Laws that are not equal to all revert to rights and privileges, something contradictory to the very nature of nation-states. The clearer the proof of their inability to treat stateless people as legal persons and the greater extension of arbitrary rule by police decree, the more difficult it is for states to resist the temptation to deprive all citizens of legal status and rule them with omnipotent police."[267] Even the imposition of economic austerity upon imperial mainstream populations, formerly buttr-essed by the spiritual deception of progressive ideological reconciliation between capitalist 'liberal-democratic' culture and socialist welfare state, omi-nously anticipates the coming insurgent tide of

---

[267] Hannah Arendt, *The Origins of Totalitarianism*, (San Diego: Harcourt Brace, 1948, 1979) p.290.

emancipatory imperatives originating from the socio-ontological underground of modernity.

Indeed, no matter how liberally inclusive or democratically conceptualized, nationalism, be it cultural or political, in all its plurality of articulations, ultimately strengthens the hegemony of a western imperialist continuum. Was this not Mandela's conundrum?[268] Contemporary nationalist social justice movements earnestly striving towards emancipatory praxis, even within a cooperative or competitive international context, are unsustainable when bereft of an insurgent trajectory capable of constituting a genuinely geonational imperative against Empire. And yet, international consciousness initially exists and unfolds from within a healthy core of national consciousness, a "two-fold emerging" that conditions insurgent potentialities against Empire initiating a socio-ontological genesis towards egalitarian geonational community as genuine world culture.[269]

A madman returns upon clouds of anguish to the now global marketplace and is heard unceasingly proclaiming that nationalism is dead. "How were we able to drink up the sea? Who gave us the sponge to wipe away the whole horizon? What did we do when we loosened this earth from its sun?

[268] Frank B. Wilderson III, *Incognegro: A Memoir of Exile & Aparteid*, (Cambridge: South End Press, 2008) pp.104-112.
[269] Fanon, *The Wretched of the Earth*, p.248.

Whither does it now move? Whither do we move? Away from all suns? Do we not dash unceasingly? Backwards, sideways, forwards, in all directions? Is there still an above and below?"[270] Telling laughter erupts amidst the bewildered herd and their new atheists, ever secure in dogmatic worship of cultural traditions and hallowed presuppositions grounded through blind faith in juridical belonging to a nationalist mythology. And yet, such well-trodden roads of modernity never lead beyond their own exacerbation of coloniality, hence positing historical progress as spiritual subservience to instrumentalist reason rooted in western imperialist power. Nationalism is dead. However, "this prodigious event is still on its way, and is travelling – it has not yet reached men's ears."[271]

Dawn has yet to break, as heavy debate in Semitic language amongst the spiritual descendants of Moorish corsairs cedes discursive primacy to the active silence required for an approaching raid in unmediated confrontation against the Leviathan of global capital, embodied in massive vessels of Empire careening through the sea off the Afroasiatic coastline. Intensely interrogating nationalist illusions, and armed with human agency, plenty of ammunition, two AK-47's, and an RPG, postmod-

---

[270] Friedrich Nietzsche, *The Gay Science*, (New York: Barnes & Noble, 1882, 2008) p.103.
[271] Nietzsche, p.104.

ern lumpenproletariat breach a geonational horizon of emancipatory praxis through inadequate piracy against western imperialist power, thus constituting an opening, a small glimpse forward, twilight beckoning towards unforeseen geonational constellations of insurrection. "Remove justice, and what are kingdoms but gangs of criminals on a large scale? What are criminal gangs but petty kingdoms? A gang is a group of men under the command of a leader, bound by a compact of association, in which the plunder is divided according to an agreed convention. If this villainy wins so many recruits from the ranks of the demoralized that it acquires territory, establishes a base, captures cities and subdues peoples, it then openly arrogates to itself the title of kingdom, which is conferred on it in the eyes of the world, not by the renouncing of aggression but by the attainment of impunity. For it was a witty and a truthful rejoinder which was given by a captured pirate to Alexander the Great. The king asked the fellow, 'What is your idea, in infesting the sea?' And the pirate answered, with uninhibited insolence, 'The same as yours, in infesting the earth! But because I do it with a tiny craft, I'm called a pirate: because you have a mighty navy, you're called emperor.'"[272]

---

[272] St. Augustine, *City of God*, (New York: Penguin Books, 426, 1972, 1984) p.139.

Nationalism is dead. Nationalist opposition to Empire, no matter how authentic and deep seeded, is ultimately assimilated by a western imperialist continuum unless it can achieve socio-historical reconstitution through geonational insurgency. Contemporary difficulties discerning emerging geonational consciousness overwhelming ideological remnants of an old world ordered in accordance to socio-historical precepts in sovereign deference to a western imperialist continuum must be overcome. For if "nationalism is not made explicit, if it is not enriched and deepened by a very rapid transformation into a consciousness of social and political needs, in other words into humanism, it leads up a blind alley."[273] This "blind alley" is now being circumnavigated by the skiffs of Afroasiatic piracy with each swashbuckling venture arrogating ransom from multinational corporations on the high seas, reminding us the sun always rises and sets upon a geonational horizon.

Geonational consciousness fuels the Return of world historical momentum to struggles of human liberation that have socio-ontologically stalled and politically collapsed under the weight of globalized hegemony as violently imposed and structurally maintained by Empire. Postmodern ambiguity towards the once unquestioned emancipatory value of

---

[273] Fanon, *The Wretched of The Earth*, p.204

electoral political representation, in correlation with juridical obligations and prerogatives of national citizenship submerged in advanced neoliberal capitalist globalization, are telling appropriate antecedents moving towards approaching geonational imperatives. For nationalism no longer issues forth as a challenge to oppression, but rather, now bereft of sovereign legitimacy, merely enunciates its stubborn acquiescence to a subordinate role of nostalgic rhetorical significance within the context of a western imperialist continuum.

Against Empire, those who seek to confront globalized oppression have but one recourse: the explicit development of geonational consciousness from which to engage in emancipatory praxis, thus revealing any proclamation of 'the end of history' as serious collusion with consistent reconfigurations of western imperialist power.

Nationalism is dead. The nation-state's capacity to fulfill its once stalwart role as sole attempted guarantor of universal human rights peaked with the Haitian revolution.[274] How can such an exemplary emancipatory history find any social reconciliation in the tragic sovereign relations currently existing between Haiti and Empire?   *Human subjectivity-as-lived universal* must liberate itself from

---

[274] C.L.R. James, *The Black Jacobins*, (New York: Vintage, 1938, 1963, 1989). Susan Buck-Morss, *Hegel, Haiti, and Universal History*, (Pittsburgh: University of Pittsburgh Press, 2009).

ideological bondage to a nationalist paradigm that perpetually replicates the geohistorical primacy of a western imperialist continuum. Any authoritative guarantee of 'inalienable rights' finds imperative existential relevance only through appeal to the Divine as transcendent horizon of meaning beyond the reach of established power.[275] However, appeals to the Divine in the absence of emancipatory praxis invite the shelter of superstition. As such, the Divine as manifest in human endeavor necessarily avoids dogmatic religious temptations of idealist mystification by its ready affirmation of universality through emancipatory praxis against Empire. For such emancipatory praxis transcends the limitations of nationalism towards a new sovereign unity of geoterritorial legitimation, thus evoking a world ordered according to a lived egalitarian cultural unity-as-diversity of geonational human community "bringing a natural rhythm into existence, introduced by new men, and with it a new language and a new humanity."[276]

The intersubjective resonance of human 'being' engaged in emancipatory praxis, reveals socio-onto-

---

[275] "In other words, in the new secular and emancipated society, men were no longer sure of these social and human rights which until then had been outside the political order and guaranteed not by government and constitution, but by social, spiritual, and religious forces." Arendt, p.291.
[276] Fanon, p.36.

logical potentialities for new constitutions of human subjectivity-as-lived universal towards a historically new "veritable creation" of egalitarian geonational community. And yet, how long can the normative gaze continue suppressing enunciations of Revolt originating from the underground of modernity? Enunciations often heard, and shared in hushed tones, then muted in cultural nationalist deference to the imperial mainstream-as-civil society, as an explicit warning against going too far, or risk bringing about the 'end of the world' through its pursuit – geonational insurrection *ad portas*.

Working Concepts, Discursive Terms & Unfixed Defintions

Alienation – process or condition of estrangement from the radical ontological freedom that characterizes human 'being'. Not to be confused with the more severe condition of dehumanization. Confronting alienation can lead to a lived experience of anguish. See **anguish, dehumanization**.

Alterity – condition of otherness as the refusal of recognition or relation of separation as the absence of reciprocity.

Anguish – lived apprehension of human 'being' as irreducible agency that is irreconcilable with the Real of any given situation. Anguish arises from the recognition that there is no substantive 'empirical self' that predetermines our actions or natural essence that justifies our behavior. Rather, there is a radical ontological freedom experienced as a kinetic distance of interiority or 'presence-towards-self' that makes us not only responsible for our actions, but also responsible for the possibility of bringing meaning to the world through our actions. Whereas dread is associated with dehumanization and the under-ground of modernity, anguish is associated with alienation and the imperial mainstream. See **alienation, dread, imperial mainstream**.

Anthropology – refers to an underlying theoretical framework and guiding discursive conception of what it means to be human.

Anti-slavery dialectic – dialectic movement of Revolt against the enslavement of human 'being' as call and response to the disaster of history.

Ascendant humanity – communities of people awakening to the emancipatory universality of their particular socio-historical struggle for liberation.

Bewildered Herd – dominated non-resisting masses as impotent before the normative gaze of established power.

Biopolitical – rooted in *chattel slavery*, the over-determination of lived experience through the regulation of bodies towards social control of populations.

Biopolitical alterity – condition of asymmetrical otherness as the systematic refusal of recognition or relation of separation as structural absence of reciprocity predicated upon objective violence accompanying mechanisms of coercion that inscribe lived relations between populations as bodies according to logics of 'race', occurring so consistently that overt racism becomes an unnecessary blemish to the prestige of established power.

Biopolitical danger – resistance so corrosive to the imperial mainstream-as-civil society that it calls into question the sovereign legitimacy of western imperialist power and thereby threatens the socio-historical stability and imperial topographical coherence of modernity. See **exceptional antagonism**.

Biopolitical pacification – exercise of power through mechanisms of coercion accompanied by objective violence towards promoting the abdication of human agency by materialist reduction of the human condition through comprehensive regulation and/or deregulation of populations as bodies according to logics of 'race', occurring so structurally consistent that overt racism becomes an unnecessary blemish to the prestige of established power.

Biopolitical persecution – regulation and/or deregulation of objective violence against bodies administered as social control and population management according to logics of 'race', occurring so structurally consistent that overt racism becomes an unnecessary blemish to the prestige of established power.

Black liberation discourse – insurgent philosophical orientation of emancipatory thought as initiated by the anti-slavery dialectic of Revolt against western imperialist power.

Black Rage – unheralded lucidity of Revolt. Piercing clarity of affective indignance as conscious-ness venturing towards voicing an incommunicable reckoning.

the Blues metaphysic – speaks to the possibility of a radical beginning as a vast reservoir of eman-cipatory creativity, imagination, aesthetics and dis-course that begins with the call and response of lived Black experience to the disaster of history as a constant improvisational search for provisional foundations of upheaval from which to approach questions of freedom, universality, justice and the human condition without recourse to equilibrium, guarantee of stability or necessity of resolution, completion or wholeness.

Civil society – exists within the imperial main-stream between public and private spheres as a terrain of rights, liberties, political consent, common interests, social influence and collective pursuits where hegemony is contested and produced while implicitly dependent on the ongoing socio-ontolo-gical stability of established power. See **imperial mainstream**.

Coercive anonymity – structurally consistent disregard of human 'being' imposed by the normative gaze of established power towards rendering particular populations 'invisible' to human consideration, ethical treatment or legal redress.

Coloniality – deterritorialized positionality of racist dehumanization as violent structural-inert relations of power inscribed within modernity itself that sustain and define lived hierarchal intermediations between imperial mainstream and socio-ontological under-ground of modernity.

Dehumanization – process or condition of reducing human 'being' to 'objecthood' as a materialist determinism that interrupts and suppresses potentialities of human agency, with the aim of establishing the foundation for a generalized withdrawal of human consideration, ethical treatment and legal redress by the normative gaze of established power. Not to be confused with the less severe condition of alienation. Confronting dehumanization can lead to a lived experience of dread. See **dread, alienation**.

the disaster – enslavement of human 'being' as the socio-ontological basis for modernity.

the Divine – absolute transcendence of the Real as unforeseen opening, sublime possibility and/or inexhaustible horizon of meaning.

Dread – lived apprehension of the human condition as irreducible agency that is irreconcilable with the Real of any given situation in the face of inevitable socio-historical persecution. What distinguishes dread from anguish is lived positionality to established power. Whereas anguish is associated with alienation and the imperial mainstream, dread is associated with dehumanization and the underground of modernity. See **dehumanization, anguish, underground of modernity**.

Emancipatory Aesthetics – emphasizes the creative tension between form of transcendence and intentionality of resistance as an aesthetic gravity that discloses emancipatory potentialities of Art.

Emancipatory praxis – conscious struggle and decisive engagement that unifies thought and action towards potentialities of human liberation.

Empire – deterritorialized sovereign legitimacy of ongoing asymmetrical reconfigurations of western imperialist power structures that are inscribed with racist dehumanization and coloniality towards globally consolidating the interests of concentrated capital as manifest in totalitarian security culture, indefinite expansion of military forces on the international front and hypermilitarization of police forces on the domestic front. See **western imperialist continuum**, **western imperialist power**.

Empirical self – materialist determinism as the substantive basis of human 'being'. See **human 'being'**.

Exceptional Antagonism – breaks through the normative gaze by radically disrupting the sovereign legitimacy of western imperialist power and thus cannot be reconciled within the prescriptive boundaries of modernity. A perpetual socio-ontological imperative towards the emancipatory possibility and universality of Revolt.

Existential liberation critique – insurgent philosophical engagement with lived Black experience that interrogates our perception of human 'being' in dynamic correlation towards conceptions of human liberation. Discursively draws upon the anti-slavery dialectic of Frederick Douglass, the existential Marxism of Jean-Paul Sartre and the decolonial phenomenology of Frantz Fanon.

Geonational – contemporary horizon of emancipatory praxis that introduces geohistorical potentialities of egalitarian social structures sustaining world community towards overcoming advanced neo-liberal capitalist globalization by transcending nation-state boundaries of an asymmetrical world ordered by a western imperialist continuum.

Hegemony – domination to the point of achieving popular legitimacy whereby even the oppressed participate through consensus in perpetuating their ongoing subjugation. See **civil society**, **imperial mainstream**.

Human 'being' – temporally embodied conscious-ness situated in the world against the Real through a kinetic distance of interiority that intro-duces radical ontological freedom as irreducible agency that is not only irreconcilable with the Real, but in constant lived intermediation against culture and history. Thus, affirmation of human 'being' realizes itself as renunciation of 'objecthood' and all attempted formulations of materialist determinism. Human 'being' is the basis of human subjectivity, but not its equivalent thereof, as human subjectivity is constituted through constantly achieving and renewing praxis without resolution towards developing a temporal and distinctive rhythm of 'being-in-the-world'. See **kinetic distance of interiority, human subjectivity.**

Human subjectivity – self-defining intentionality that arises from human 'being' as resistance against the Real and lived intermediation with temporality, culture and history. Human subjectivity is constituted and continuously reconstituted through lived rhythm of praxis as simultaneous movement towards the world and intersubjective resonance towards one another.

Identity – locates and secures a substantive 'empirical self' through stable positionality to the Real and harmonious relation to the normative gaze of established power. Identity mediates against the irreducibility of human agency and as such, is a furtive achievement of human 'being', not the equivalent of human subjectivity, though it shares the same basis. See **empirical self**, **human 'being'**, **human subjectivity**.

Ideology – epistemic closure and cultural reification of a particular system of thought as absolute. Ideology is generated by the normative gaze of established power. See **normative gaze**.

Imperial mainstream – globally designated cosmopolitan populations that merit human consideration, ethical treatment and legal redress according to the normative gaze of Empire based on race, class or nationality. See **civil society**.

Imperial topography – superimposed asymmetrical positionality of the imperial mainstream over the socio-ontological underground of modernity as a rational coherence and hierarchal arrangement of historical features and cultural consolidations of western imperialist power. Implicitly represents the natural order of the world according to the normative gaze of modernity. See **positionality**.

Insurgent philosophy – emancipatory thought that interrogates the Real and enunciates Revolt from the underground of modernity at the crossroads of Truth, meaning and power.

Insurrection-for-itself – organized intentionality and lived experience of revolutionary struggle as disciplined social movement towards reopening history to potentialities of human liberation.

Insurrection-in-itself – lived dynamic unity of protest-as-resistance and spontaneous rebellion as unregulated social movement towards reopening history to potentialities of human liberation.

Intersubjective resonance – metaphysics of heightened reciprocity generated by close proximity between one human 'being' and another that reverberates with constitutive significance and potentialities towards human subjectivity and community by evoking the prospect of adversity as a catalyst of movement towards unity or towards conflict.

Kinetic distance of interiority – threefold dynamic of consciousness as *constitutive self-determination* (consciousness introduces meaning to the world), *relentless transcendence* (consciousness surpasses the situated present) and *spiritual upheaval* (consciousness uproots the constituted past) that discloses the human condition as always already a continuous 'presence-towards-self' rather than an 'empirical self'. see **human 'being'**.

Lived rhythm of praxis – self-defining intention-ality and temporal movement towards the world and intersubjective resonance towards one another as the trajectory of human 'being' that constitutes human subjectivity. see **human subjectivity**. see **praxis**.

Lived universal – metaphysics of dynamic unity and universal relevance achieved through singularity of lived experience.

Miseducation of soul – epistemological indoctrination and ideological coercion towards abdicating the irreducible agency of human 'being' in favor of objecthood, rational animality or a fixed 'empirical self' as modes of materialist determinism. Miseducation of soul works in tandem with objective violence towards constituting the normative gaze. See **normative gaze**, **ideology**.

Modernity – contemporary post-traditional social structures accompanying the nation-state as historically imposed through an ongoing praxis of imperial conquest, genocide, colonial expansion, industrial revolution and human slavery, while ideologically proclaiming belief in evolutionary social progress, scientific rationality, democracy, technological advancement, human rights, mass production, standardization, division of labor, urbanization and economic development. Although modernity is often associated with the decline of religion, it would be more accurate to suggest that modernity merely introduced Race, Nation and Capital as a new pantheon of gods that now easily compete with and often eclipse the Cause of God in terms of authentic religious devotion.

Neo-colonial policing – counterinsurgent use of domestic police force as an occupying army to manage local populations and subjugate nascent potentialities of Revolt through hypermilitarization, civic initiatives and zero tolerance measures towards preserving socio-ontological boundaries between the imperial mainstream and the underground of modernity.

the Normative gaze – unreflective ideological background framework and socio-ontological filter towards ensuring that everyday people *see* themselves, *look* at one another and *engage* the world almost exclusively from the sanctioned perspectives of established power. The normative gaze is constituted through objective violence and miseducation of soul, preempting both the enunciation of spontaneous thought in ordinary discourse and the articulation of formal rationality in academia.

Objecthood – ultimate aim or condition of dehumanization that reduces human 'being' to a materialist determinism that interrupts and suppresses potentialities of human agency, so as to establish a foundation for maintaining a generalized withdrawal of human consideration, ethical treatment and legal redress from the normative gaze of established power. See **dehumanization**.

Objective violence – structural-inert violence sanctioned by established power that reproduces its sovereign legitimacy and reaches such a repetitive degree of systemic frequency that it rationally escapes social notice and historical scrutiny out of sheer familiarity. Objective violence works in tandem with miseducation of soul towards constituting the normative gaze. See **normative gaze, structural-inert**.

Ontology – questions fundamental structures of being, existence and reality. Focuses on '*what* there really is' rather than '*that* there actually is'.

Overdetermination-from-without – coercive interventions towards supplanting human subjectivity by imposing 'objecthood' upon human 'being' as a fixed identity based on constant external reinforcement by the normative gaze of established power. See **normative gaze, identity**.

Phenomenology – questions experience through the direct immediacy of that which appears before consciousness. Focuses on '*that* there actually is' rather than '*what* there really is'.

Positionality – lived hierarchal correlation of human 'being' to the topographical coherence of established power as constituted by the normative gaze, often the basis of identity. See **Identity**, **imperial topography**.

Postmodern lumpenproletariat – emancipatory unity of race, class and international outcasts arising from both imperial mainstream and socio-ontological underground of modernity against Empire towards introducing the possibility of geonational egalitarian community.

Praxis – conscious struggle and decisive engagement that unifies thought and action towards introducing meaning into the world. Consistent praxis develops a temporal rhythm that often serves as the initial basis for constituting human subjectivity out of the radical ontological freedom of human 'being'. Praxis can also refer to systematic action organized by established power towards constituting the Real. See **lived rhythm of praxis.** See **human subjectivity**.

Precipice of Anomie – socio-ontological crossroads of lived positionality where power exists in an ethical and legal indeterminacy. The sovereign legitimacy of western imperialist power is constituted through the precipice of anomie as it structures existing hierarchal relations between imperial mainstream and the underground of modernity. The imperial mainstream experiences the precipice of anomie when established power makes declarations of a 'State of Emergency' during which civil rights are officially suspended towards preserving the stability of established power as the condition of possibility for civil society. However, the stability of civil society is experienced as an unrelenting socio-ontological gravity of structural-inert violence by the underground of modernity, for whom, the precipice of anomie constitutes an ongoing and undeclared 'State of Emergency' that distinguishes imperial mainstream from the underground of modernity in the name of law and order. As such, for the underground of modernity, even the *form* of civil rights collapses as a pretense that enables the *fact* of civil rights to be negated as perpetually called into question by the normative gaze of established power.

Presence-towards-self – kinetic distance of interiority that characterizes the human condition as temporally situated consciousness. See **kinetic distance of interiority**. See **Human 'being'**. See **Human Subjectivity.**

Protest-as-resistance – disturbing the sovereign legitimacy of the normative gaze by an ascendant humanity that confronts established power with an emancipatory gaze of Revolt. Willing to disrespect and disregard the boundaries of civil society in the name of Justice.

Protest-as-ritual event – reduction of protest to liberal-democratic passion plays that function more as catharsis for the imperial mainstream rather than as effective resistance by the underground of modernity to established power. Willing to respect and uphold the boundaries of civil society in the name of law and order.

Race – rational signification of subhumanity masquerading as a neutral category to classify the intrinsic wealth of diversity and radical ontological freedom that characterizes the human condition, towards a stabilization of human 'being' into a fixed order of materialist determinism and hierarchal identity in service to western imperialist power.

Rational animality – subordination of the irreducible agency of human 'being' to the absolute limitations of biological determinism.

the Raw – metaphysics of the extreme as lived intensity and/or binding proximity.

the Real – non-conscious plenitude and exhaustive materiality of existence that is drenched in culture and history and thus both situates the human condition and mediates against it.

Reciprocity – mutual recognition, dependence, action or influence.

the Return – metaphysics of consequence. The blowback of oppression returning to source through diverse means of intermediation and/or modes of emancipatory praxis.

Revolt – phenomenon that introduces ontological significance to socio-historical rebellion.

Socio-ontological – refers to binding questions of socio-historical relevance and ontological consequence.

Structural-inert – structural embodiment of praxis as passively comprehensible.

Underground of modernity – the wretched of the earth. Race, class and international outcasts condemned by a western imperialist continuum to suffer through coloniality as a perpetually underdeveloped, underprivileged, undereducated, underrepresented, underclass of modernity and who therefore merit no human consideration, ethical treatment or legal redress under the normative gaze of established power.

Vertigo of emancipatory praxis – consciousness realizing itself as inebriating movement of dis-equilibrium towards rupturing the normative gaze through engaging in emancipatory praxis.

Western imperialist continuum – socio-historical continuity of a comprehensively administered power structure of racist dehumanization and coloniality in all its varied manifestations and consistent reconfigurations spanning from European invasions of the Americas, beginning in 1492 on through today in our contemporary world of advanced neo-liberal capitalist globalization. See **Empire**.

Western imperialist power – socio-historical imposition of a heavily administered power structure of racist dehumanization and coloniality permeated by geopolitical imperatives of domination and exploitation through concentrated capital, indefinite expansion of military forces on the international front and hypermilitarization of police on the home front. See **Empire**.

Wretched of the earth – the socio-ontological underground of modernity. Race, class and international outcasts. See **underground of modernity**.

CANNAE
PRESS

****